Creative Approaches to Teaching Primary RE

OXFORD BROOKES
UNIVERSITY
LIBRARY

D0488598

PEARSON

We work with leading authors to develop the strongest
educational materials in teaching and education, bringing
cutting-edge thinking and best learning practice to a
global market.

Under a range of well-known imprints, including
Longman, we craft high quality print and electronic
publications which help readers to understand
and apply their content, whether studying or at work.

To find out more about the complete range of our
publishing please visit us on the World Wide Web at:
www.pearsoned.co.uk

Creative Approaches to Teaching Primary RE

Maggie Webster
Edge Hill University

Longman
is an imprint of

Harlow, England • London • New York • Boston • San Francisco • Toronto • Sydney • Singapore • Hong Kong
Tokyo • Seoul • Taipei • New Delhi • Cape Town • Madrid • Mexico City • Amsterdam • Munich • Paris • Milan

Pearson Education Limited
Edinburgh Gate
Harlow
Essex CM20 2JE
England

and Associated Companies throughout the world

Visit us on the World Wide Web at:
www.pearsoned.co.uk

First published 2010

ACC. NO. 953673 06   FUND CDUG
LOC. ET   CATEGORY week   PRICE £22.99
13 DEC 2012
CLASS No. 372.84 WEB
OXFORD BROOKES UNIVERSITY LIBRARY

© Pearson Education Limited 2010

The right of Maggie Webster to be identified as author of this work has been asserted by her in accordance with the Copyright, Designs and Patents Act 1988.

All rights reserved. No part of this publication may be reproduced, stored in a retrieval system, or transmitted in any form or by any means, electronic, mechanical, photocopying, recording or otherwise, without either the prior
written permission of the publisher or a licence permitting restricted copying in the United Kingdom issued by the Copyright Licensing Agency Ltd, Saffron House, 6–10 Kirby Street, London EC1N 8TS.

All trademarks used herein are the property of their respective owners. The use of any trademark in this text does not vest in the author or publisher any trademark ownership rights in such trademarks, nor does the use of such trademarks imply any affiliation with or endorsement of this book by such owners.

ISBN: 978-1-4082-0440-5

British Library Cataloguing-in-Publication Data
A catalogue record for this book is available from the British Library

Library of Congress Cataloging-in-Publication Data
A catalog record for this book is available from the Library of Congress

10 9 8 7 6 5 4 3 2 1
13 12 11 10 09

Typeset in 30 by Pantek Arts Ltd, Maidstone, Kent
Printed and bound in Geat Britain by Ashford Colour Press Ltd, Gosport, Hants

The publisher's policy is to use paper manufactured from sustainable forests.

I would like to dedicate this book to

My Mum and Dad for always making me sing *I've got confidence* when I lose faith!

Michaela, Anita and Eirwen for your unwavering loyalty towards me

Darren who started me on the road to self-discovery

M and J who frequently walk that road to help me clarify my ideas

And to my loving husband Alan. Your belief and trust in me is astounding!

God Bless you all. Thank you.

Brief Contents

Contents

About the author

Courtesy of Stuart Rayner **www.stuartrayner.com**

Maggie started her NQT career in East London in 1995. During this time she was an RE and Collective Worship coordinator and a member of Newham's SACRE. She was part of a working party to review and rewrite the Religious Education syllabus.

She became a bilingual support teacher in 1998 and in 2000 became a Project Manager and Museum Educator for The British Library (the largest museum library in the UK) where she managed a DfES funded project called *Words Alive!* Maggie's focus was to explore the collection to create thematic and cross-curricular Literacy activities, which she then tested with eight schools in Camden and seven schools in Torbay. The workshops were adapted and then put onto a website at www.blewa.co.uk.

In 2002 Maggie became a Literacy Consultant for St Helens Education Action Zone, and worked with three secondary schools and thirteen primary schools developing cross-curricular projects, which encouraged creative thinking in Literacy lessons.

In 2004–2005 she did voluntary work with a primary school in Uganda West Africa for five weeks and then developed global awareness projects that lasted 18 months with schools in Merseyside, which ended with an exhibition in the World of Glass Museum in St Helens.

Maggie now works as a Senior Lecturer in Edge Hill University's Primary Education department and is a course leader for Children's Development and Learning and can be seen on Teachers' TV (www.teachers.tv/video/30177) delivering a lecture about English as an additional language.

Preface

To all who are passionately dedicated to the search for new 'epiphanies' of beauty so that through their creative work as artists they may offer these gifts to the world

His Holiness Pope John Paul II
Source: Letter to Artists (1999) Libreria Editrice Vaticana, 1999 © Libreria Editrice Vaticana

Why read this book?

The purpose of this book is not to change your opinion of what creativity is or what should be taught in Religious Education; it is to help you begin to think why RE is a relevant subject that should be included in the ever-changing curriculum and to help you think of ways you can creatively teach it in accordance with your own personality and teaching style.

My husband (a Geography teacher of 15 years) said to me that the reason he still reads books about education is so that he can think about his situation from a different perspective and keep a fresh approach to his teaching. Trainee teachers have said to me that they pick up a text so that they can gain some top tips for teaching, find a good quote for an essay and pass with a good grade! Whichever reason you have for choosing this book, its aim is for you to use it to help you formulate new opinions, new ways of looking at things and also, at times, for you to agree or disagree with the author. This way you will consolidate the pedagogy that you believe to be true and thus become a more reflective practitioner.

Maggie Webster

Acknowledgements

Author's acknowledgement

Thanks to all the children from Our Lady's and St Edwards Roman Catholic Primary School, Preston.

Publisher's acknowledgements

We are grateful to the following for permission to reproduce copyright material:

Figures

Illustration on cover, page xviii and in colour plate section from Catherine Brogna, Year 5, Brunshaw Primary School, Burnley, Lancashire; Figure 9.1 adapted from *Forms of Assessment in Religious Education: The main report from the FARE project*, FARE Project, Exeter (Copley, T. and Priestly, J. 1991) p. 140, Reproduced by permission of the FARE project, University of Exeter School of Education and Lifelong Learning; Figure 9.2 adapted from *Forms of Assessment in Religious Education: The main report from the FARE project*, FARE Project, Exeter (Copley, T. and Priestly, J. 1991) p. 140, Reproduced by permission of the FARE project, University of Exeter School of Education and Lifelong Learning; Figure 10.2 adapted from *Teaching Thinking Skills Across the Primary School*, David Fulton Publishers (B. Wallace 2001) Routledge (UK) (part of Taylor & Francis)/Cengage/Thomson.

Photograph

Photograph on page xiii from Stuart Rayner www.stuartrayner.com.

Screenshots

Screenshot on page 76 from University of Cumbria; Screenshot on page 94 from Articles of Faith.

Text

Extract on page xv from Letter to Artists (1999) Libreria Editrice Vaticana, 1999 © Libreria Editrice Vaticana; Case Study on pages 29–31 adapted from The act of creation, *Teaching Thinking and Creativity*, 9(2), pp. 6–11 (Chamberlain, A. and Northcott, M. 2009), Imaginative Minds; Extracts on page 4, page 7, page 100 from *Religious Education: The non-statory framework*, QCA (Qualifications and Curriculum Authority 2004) QCA.

In some instances we have been unable to trace the owners of copyright material, and we would appreciate any information that would enable us to do so.

Illlustration by Catherine Brogna

Chapter 1
What is creative education?

LEARNING OBJECTIVES

In this chapter we will consider:

- The definition of creativity
- How to learn creatively
- How creativity is demonstrated
- The definition of creative Religious Education

It will also address elements within the following Standards:

Q8, Q10, Q14, Q15, Q18, Q29

Introduction: What is creativity?

Creativity is subjective. What one person considers to be creative another may find unimaginative or mundane. For instance, the shortlist for the Tate Modern's Turner Prize provokes much controversy each year. Damien Hirst's *Mother and Child, Divided* won the prize in 1995 and *My Bed* by Tracey Emin was short-listed in 1999, yet both occasioned considerable discussion in the press and amongst many ordinary people about whether they were even art. Many considered that a cow cut in half and preserved in formaldehyde and a bed that looked similar to most people's on a Sunday morning lacked creativity and were either far too elitist, or far too mundane, to be seen as good art (Turpin, 1995; Robson, 1999). However, the Turner Prize judges (along with other acclaimed art critics) considered both to be imaginative, creative and inspiring originals, thus proving that creativity is a matter of personal taste and bias.

If creativity is personal and educational learning has become prescribed through the National Curriculum and National Strategies, it seems that 'The Creative Curriculum', a general term which is used by many, including the National College of School Leadership (www.ncsl.org.uk) and The Arts Council (www.artscouncil.org.uk), is an oxymoron (Burgess, 2007). Education has, for a long time, lost its personal touch and the curriculum has become pigeon-holed to focus on English and Mathematics; categorising what a child should be learning in each term and at each level. Individuality, either that of the teacher or the class, has been squeezed out in an attempt to raise the standards of those who are generally considered the middle ability children. Yet, since the *Excellence and Enjoyment* document (DfES, 2003), the *Rose Review* (Rose, 2008) and the *Cambridge Primary Review* (Curtis, 2009) creativity is a concept that is becoming more fashionable within the fields of education and there seems to be a broad but loosely agreed definition of what it is.

The National Advisory Committee on Creative and Cultural Education (NACCCE) considers cross-curricular teaching to be a creative approach to learning that is within us all and develops self esteem (1999:6), whereas other organisations such as Creative Partnerships (www.creative-partnerships.com) extend the definition to include learning through a skills-based programme mainly through and with the arts, i.e. dance, drama, music. However, there seem to be two separate concepts: learning creatively and being creative. *Learning creatively* is the mode of learning, i.e. how a person learns in a certain environment, whereas *being creative* is how a person may demonstrate what they have learnt through a creative method.

Learning creatively

Since 2003, the education climate has seemed to encourage us to become more creative or experimental in our teaching. Terms such as *Personalised Learning*; *Visual Auditory and Kinaestheic Learning* (VAK); *Personal Learning and Thinking Skills* (PLTS) and *Brain Gym* offer what are considered by some to be new and innovative approaches to learning (Mansell, 2008; Taylor, 11 January 2008; Mansell *et al.*, 2008) and this does not seem to be solely a Primary issue.

In 2002, the Department for Education and Skills (DfES) provided guidance on how to make the Key Stage 3 curriculum more adaptable so as to improve pupil attainment and interest (DfES, 2002). Since then, the DfES has morphed into the Department for Children,

Schools and Families (DCSF) and stated that from September 2008 schools in England would have more autonomy to create an integrated Key Stage 3 curriculum (www.qca.org.uk). They advocate a more flexible approach to learning and teaching, thereby proving that creative teaching is beginning to be seen as the X factor that can turn a child off or on to learning.

Indeed, throughout 2008 the *TES*, *The Guardian* newspaper and many authorities on educational issues such as Escalate (http://escalate.ac.uk/) have produced book reviews and articles about creativity and the curriculum. They discuss how to teach creative lessons using an interactive skills-based approach and suggest that, because children learn in a holistic way, they should learn through a variety of subjects so that they are able to explore the imaginative and creative parts of the brain. The National Curriculum in Action website (www.ncaction.org.uk/creativity) dedicates 11 web pages, which include video clips, to helping you understand what the Qualifications and Curriculum Authority (QCA) consider creativity to be and how to plan for it, suggesting that learning and teaching creatively should be a key priority for you and the school you work in.

Being creative

However, demonstrating creativity still needs to be considered. Exam pressure, and SATs in particular, have undermined many of the opportunities to explore the creative part of the brain and, possibly due to league tables, some schools have opted to teach towards a measurable target that indicates what a child has learnt in a narrow field. I would argue that because it is not mandatory to measure creativity, it is not a requirement to demonstrate it, which is a shame.

Since the new millennium, the Government has been trying to consider children's individual creativity and find a way of targeting their progress. They are doing this through registering Gifted and Talented (G&T) pupils within schools or with a G&T Academy (the National Academy for Gifted and Talented Youth) and by appointing school coordinators to monitor the academic progress of their identified G&T children (www.qca.org.uk/qca_1972apsx). A school is required to provide opportunities to enhance a child's individual talent or gift in something at which they excel, and enjoyable activities such as external visits, holiday schools or extended work within the classroom suggest that frequent testing of such children and a prescribed curriculum has not stopped them learning through a creative medium or inhibited their creative expression. But there still seem to be few opportunities for the average Jo and Jenny Bloggs to explore and develop their individual creative talents within the ordinary classroom.

Thus, we need not only constantly to teach in a creative way to explore ideas and maintain motivation, but also to provide opportunities for **all** children to express what they know and understand in a way that they choose, so that there is opportunity for their creativity to be encouraged. If children are permitted to express their understanding in a method they prefer, rather than one which is prescribed, then creativity will be enhanced. This way the child is more likely to develop the creative potential that is compatible with their personality and interests; for not all children enjoy expressing themselves through art, dance, drama or music, some prefer to explore their understanding through writing, discussions or a presentation. Therefore, as creativity is subjective, it is crucial that the child be offered an opportunity to demonstrate their learning in a way that **they** consider to be creative and not through a way you consider it should be revealed.

Measuring creativity

Creativity is something that is unique to each individual. As such, it is difficult to measure through an agreed set of targets such as Level Descriptors. Yet Attainment Targets still need to be evaluated so that children are provided with the chance to explore increasingly difficult skills and develop both sides of the brain and, as Howard Gardner (1993) would agree, this should happen by being given the opportunity to investigate a variety of intelligences. That is why you need to provide creative opportunities for all children to examine what they know and understand through a teaching method that not only stimulates, motivates and interests your class and yourself as a professional, but also encourages the children you teach to probe the creative gene within themselves. One size for creativity does not fit all and so creative education is the chance to learn through an environment that encourages personal expression of one's own view of the world. This is not easy to measure, yet the fact that it cannot be easily quantified does not mean it should not be catered for.

What is creative Religious Education?

Exploring the world we live in is a fundamental concept of religion, and enquiring into how people live their lives is one of the ways that a child can begin to develop their own opinion on how society works. Religious Education can support a child's growing understanding of themselves, their belief systems and how they fit into the society in which they live. Creative RE is crucial in allowing children to practise enquiry skills, thinking skills, listening skills and communication skills so that they develop an understanding of themselves and others (see Chapter 3).

Creativity can be encouraged in many ways through RE and, as we have seen, because creativity is subjective and involves the expression of a child's own opinion, RE is perfectly placed to support it. Within the Non Statutory Framework, Attainment Target 2 (AT2) Learning *from* Religion, encourages pupils to develop

> *reflection on, and response to, their own experiences and learning about religion. It develops pupils' skills of application, interpretation and evaluation of what they learn about religion, particularly questions of identity and belonging, meaning, purpose, truth, values and commitments.*
> (QCA, 2004:34)

These skills are essential for the development of creative thinking, as they encourage the expression of a personal viewpoint. A further noted skill of 'Communicating their responses' (ibid.) advocates personal interpretation, which gives the pupils scope to present what they know and understand through any means they choose.

Moreover, Attainment Target 1 (AT1), Learning *about* religion, encourages communication, while focusing mainly on skills that develop the retention of knowledge, i.e. through enquiry, analysis and interpretation. So, if you teach AT1 and AT2 together, you will ensure a two-pronged approach to creativity and holistic learning. For the children in your class to have the opportunity to *learn creatively* and *be creative* they need the opportunity to be taught the aims of Religious Education because, by its innate characteristics, RE encourages both internal enquiry and the external expression of creativity.

Creative Religious Education lessons offer children the opportunity to explore the 'What', the 'Why' and the 'So what?' of how people choose to live their lives. For this reason it needs to be considered seriously in schools. Without the opportunity to contemplate collective and individual answers to personal questions and discuss what they mean in society, bigotry and racism are likely to abound.

To develop creativity in children, you need to open up your professional imagination and enable your class to delve into the creative learning process. Creative learning and teaching with creative interpretation are the essential ingredients of RE and how and why to do this are explored in Chapters 3 to 8.

Summary of key points

- Creativity is subjective
- The Government is encouraging all teachers to be creative in their teaching and learning
- Creativity needs nurturing through allowing children to demonstrate what they know and understand in their **own preferred style**
- There is a difference between learning creatively and being creative
- RE is well positioned to be an excellent vehicle for creativity

Chapter 2
The purpose of Religious Education

LEARNING OBJECTIVES

In this chapter we will consider:

- The current purpose of Religious Education
- Historical events that have impacted on RE in schools
- Current and past legislation relating to RE
- The difference between RI and RE
- How, when society changes, so does RE in schools

It will also address elements within the following Standards:

Q3, Q15, Q21

Introduction: What is the purpose of RE today?

In today's over-subscribed curriculum, and given the constant pressures of new initiatives, it is difficult to find time to teach all the subjects that are required in a primary school. Religious Education can at times be a subject that is marginalised (Revell, 2005) and one of the first subjects you may not teach if you have to make a choice between achieving good SAT results or completing a unit of work for a core subject. There are many reasons why RE goes first, yet it is mainly because of the many insecurities you may feel due to lack of knowledge or understanding about its role in a child's holistic education.

It is necessary then for you to reflect on what you think the purpose of Religious Education is, especially in a society where religion is receiving increasingly bad press. It seems that many people consider religion to be a reason for hatred and war, so it is important for you as a professional to address the question of whether religion and the subject of Religious Education have a place in schools.

In the *Non Statutory Framework for Religious Education*, Charles Clarke (the former Education Secretary) states that, 'Good-quality religious education can transform pupils' assessment of themselves and others, and their understanding of the wider position of the world in which we live.' (QCA, 2004:3) This is the main purpose of RE in the twenty-first century: to ensure that children have the opportunity to consider who they are, what they believe and how they want to live; and it is your responsibility to facilitate their enquiries.

Yet the purpose of RE has changed over the years and it now has a distinctive aim to encourage personal reflection and enquiry into the six major faith traditions that are represented in Great Britain. Historically it has not possessed such an open-minded approach.

A brief history of the changing role of Religious Education in schools

Religion and education seem to have been bedfellows since 1780, when church schools were begun by Thomas Stocks and Robert Raikes in 1777 and 1780, respectively. During this time, education seemed to be set up as a way to offer moral direction to disorderly children and it is interesting to note that, as society changes, so does the attitude to Religious Education in schools.

For example, the impact of racist attitudes on the ethnic groups arriving in the 1950s made it imperative to educate children into multicultural awareness (http://www.national archives.gov.uk/pathways/citizenship/brave_new_world/immigration.htm). In more recent times, the aftermath to 9/11 has been devastating for Muslims as they were targeted by the general public in the United States and UK and so became victims of hate crimes (http://news.bbc.co.uk/1/hi/uk/1576854.stm). In some cases, Sikhs have been attacked after being mistaken for Islamic extremists; on 15 September 2001 a Sikh petrol station owner in Arizona was killed for that reason (*Times of India* 2001 http://timesofindia.indiatimes.com/articleshoe/1723325485.cms). Such incidents prove that there has long been a need for society in general to be aware of religious practice in order to avoid bigotry and racial hatred (BBC News 2001).

These and similar incidents have encouraged interfaith dialogue between religious leaders and communities and such discussions have since had an effect on RE syllabi in schools and Local Authorities. The purpose of Religious Education in schools has evolved to become a means to understanding and respecting difference, as well as encouraging integration.

The 1944 Act

It was during the 1940s that the Government began seriously to address the state of education in schools. Prior to 1944, government posts in education were deemed relatively unimportant, particularly in wartime Britain. In 1941, then Prime Minister Winston Churchill appointed Richard Austin (Rab) Butler to the position of President of the Board of Education. Authorised by Churchill to make changes to the education system, Rab Butler introduced the 1944 Education Act (often known as the Butler Education Act). As well as creating the Ministry of Education (with Butler as the first Minister of Education), the Act was to prove hugely influential on the future education system.

In terms of Religious Instruction (RI), the 1870 Elementary Education Act had stipulated that religious teaching in board schools should be restricted to non-denominational teaching, or none at all. Furthermore, parents had the right to withdraw their children from religious education; and this applied even to church schools. Schools that were supported by ratepayers' money were actually prohibited from using distinctive religious systems.

The Butler Education Act went a long way to improving the previous system. For the first time, Christian churches and the Government were openly recognised as equal education and financial partners (Acts of Parliament, 1944). And in general terms, the Act stated that:

- Religious Instruction (RI) should happen at least once a week, the content of which should be based on an agreed syllabus created by the Local Authority.

- Every Local Authority should have a Standing Advisory Council for Religious Education (SACRE), which should monitor RI in schools.

- RI should be regularly inspected, as it was now compulsory in schools alongside a daily act of worship.

Although much of the specified RI content of the Act was already being taught in schools under the guise of Moral Education and Christian Education, it wasn't until 1944 that RI was made compulsory; had syllabi attached and required inspection. This top–down change was due mainly to the Government's view that the provision of moral guidance was needed to counteract changing social values and the disintegration of the family unit, both direct results of the Second World War.

The content of many syllabi was Scripture, as it was considered the starting point for many denominations and seemed to focus more on religious knowledge than on religious understanding. RI was promoted as an academic subject that used many skills similar to that of English. However, RI and the Act had a contradictory message commonly known as the 'Conscience Clause', which originated in the 1870 Elementary Education Act and which started a discussion about timetabling a place for children whose parents wished them not to take part in any form of religious instruction in the school (Louden, 2003). The contradiction was that, although Religious Instruction had been made compulsory, a parent could still remove their child from the lessons on religious grounds. Such a clause seemed to undermine RI's academic and equal status with other subjects, for a child could not be removed from English lessons.

By the mid 1950s, educationalists had come to disagree on the content of RI, some arguing that it did not yet reflect changing social values: RI was being taught as a way to instruct every child into the Christian faith, even if the child was one of the many Sikhs who had immigrated to the UK from India. By the end of the 1950s and early 1960s, however, Local Education Authority syllabi began to address issues such as ethnicity and started providing examples of plans that suggested methods which encouraged religious enquiry.

By 1966, the West Riding syllabus had been created, which advocated thematic, child-centred teaching (Hull, 1990; West Riding County of Yorkshire, 1966) and in 1969 the Christian Education Movement (CEM http://www.christianeducation.org.uk) organised an interfaith meeting at the village of Shap in the Lake District, which resulted in the production of various religious materials. The syllabi advocated a variety of teaching and learning opportunities that would develop exploration into religious issues, not simply instruction into Christianity.

In the 1970s, this discussion was extended, starting with *The Fourth R*, a report commissioned by the Church of England Board of Education and the National Society and produced in 1970 by the Commission on Religious Education in Schools. This looked at the provision of Religious Instruction in schools and argued for replacing the concept of RI with RE (1970:274). After consulting widely with various religious leaders, including Secular and Humanist societies, the report recommended dedicating at least two periods a week to Religious Education and stressed that the role of the subject was not instruction into one faith, but exploration of personal belief systems, and thus it should be part of the general education programme offered in schools (1970:277, 278). However, throughout the 1970s there was opposition to the change in focus of RI in schools, as some stated that the teaching was not in tune with the requirements of the 1944 Act.

In contrast to the 1970s, there was little controversy in the early to mid 1980s. In 1985, the Swann Report highlighted the importance of the child at the centre of RE and stressed that they should be seen as a valuable resource (Swann, 1985). Also in 1985, the PCfRE (Professional Council for RE) was created, which produced magazines (*REtoday* and *REsource*) for schools. These remain popular publications covering educational ideas, plans and general research for teachers interested in Christian education and religion in general (www.retoday.org.uk).

By the 1980s, the Department for Education and Skills (DES) had grown to become a large department employing over 50,000 staff; thus the Education Minister's job had evolved since Butler's time to become an important role in Government. A new Education Reform Act became legislation in 1988 and was the outcome of the so-called 'Great Debate' initiated by James Callaghan's speech at John Ruskin College in 1976 (Woodward, 2005; Callaghan, 1976). The 1988 Education Reform Act was intended to address the issues of accountability, raised by Callaghan and other politicians, and shake up the education system, making schools accountable to the taxpayers.

The 1988 Act

The 1988 Education Reform Act introduced the National Curriculum, and Kenneth Baker (then Secretary of State for Education and Science) felt that, while Religious Education should be compulsory, it should not be part of the National Curriculum (Copley, 1997). When the Bill reached the House of Lords, however, many felt that RE was being marginalised by placing it outside the National Curriculum. Baker explained that RE had to sit alongside the National Curriculum because the churches did not want the content of RE to be decided by the National Curriculum Council (a secular body) who decided the content of the other subjects. As every Local Education Authority (LEA) had a different ethnic makeup, the churches wanted each LEA, with their Standing Advisory Council for Religious Education (SACRE), to decide the content of their individual curricula, which would be produced through an LEA syllabus. Although it was acknowledged that RE had status and was part of the basic curriculum, the House of Lords was still unhappy with this reasoning (ibid.).

The resulting Bill stipulated that RE should be taught alongside the other subjects in the National Curriculum and that as the country was 85 per cent Christian, most of the content would be Christian-based; the other faith traditions would still be represented, but would not be given as much time. Every Local Education Authority had to have a SACRE, who would create and review their syllabi every five years; thus the purpose of RE was related to the societal needs and makeup of each Authority. 'The Conscience Clause' of 1870 and 1944, however, remained.

Society changed again in the 1990s. Churches began applying to the National Lottery for funding for the upkeep of buildings, suggesting that there was a problem with finances due to the decline in church attendance, despite church statistics maintaining that there were still close to 1 million regular attendees. However, media such as the *Church Times* in 1993 showed a divide in the Church of England over the ordination of women priests. Some priests were so upset with the idea of agreeing to ordain women that they resigned or converted to Roman Catholicism. Society's changing values seemed to be having an effect on religious practice and, in general, began to take a more 'pick-and-mix' approach to religion. There were many debates about whether Christianity was on the decline and whether people felt that any significance the Church might have was predominantly symbolic or historical (Copley, 1997:156).

However, although Religious Education in schools was still not held in particularly high regard during this time, events such as the abduction, torture and murder in Bootle of a 2-year-old-boy named James Bulger by Jon Venables and Robert Thompson who were both aged 10 at the time (http://news.bbc.co.uk/onthisday/hi/dates/stories/february/20/newsid_2552000/ 2552185.stm) raised questions about how schools could encourage spiritual and moral learning through Religious Education lessons. The 1990s therefore focused on research into new ways of approaching RE pedagogy through syllabi, resources and schemes of work.

The Qualification and Curriculum Authority (formerly the School Curriculum and Assessment Authority – SCAA) produced a model syllabus in 1993 whereby different members of religious communities came together to create a good example of what should be taught to children throughout the Key Stages (http://re-xs.ucsm.ac.uk/pgce/otherdocs.html). The model syllabus was to be used by LEAs as a guide, for it had become apparent from inspections that RE provision varied from Authority to Authority. Model 1 was named *Living Faiths Today* and Model 2 *Questions and Teachings* (SCAA Working Groups, 1993). They produced two Attainment Targets that, when taught together, encouraged children to develop knowledge about different religions as well as also exploring personal attitudes and beliefs. The models identified skills such as interpretation, reflection and empathy and encouraged a skills-based approach to learning.

The purpose of RE at this time was to educate children so that they learnt about and from religion (SCAA Working Groups, 1993:5), but its provision varied across the country. In 1993, 98 out of 107 SACRE inspection reports were collated to provide an overview of the general learning and teaching of RE throughout England (SCAA, 1994). The outcomes in 1993 and 1994 showed that there was no equity of learning experience and provision of RE throughout the different Local Authorities. The main reasons for this were losing an advisory teacher in RE or not having one; general funding cuts; shortage of specialist teachers and a general lack of awareness of the syllabus and its requirements.

In 2004, an attempt was made to address some of the uneven provision by producing the *Non Statutory Framework for Religious Education* (QCA, 2004). It was designed to be an extension of the 1993 SCAA model syllabus, with a similar layout to the new National Curriculum of 1999. It made progress explicit through the use of Level Descriptors and also emphasised the importance of assessment within the subject. Schools and RE professionals have received this document favourably, as it has brought greater clarification of what should be taught. Although LEAs still differ on the content of their own syllabi, on the whole they have followed this guide to create, enhance or improve them.

The millennium

It could be suggested, however, that it was at the start of the new millennium that the most important debate to date took place, which changed society's view of religion. Following Victoria Climbié's death in 2000 (http://www.victoria-climbie-inquiry.org.uk/) and the subsequent *Every Child Matters* agenda (http://www.everychildmatters.gov.uk), schools have paid more heed to the rights of the child and the pupil voice and this has been evident through trends in educational legislation and RE schemes of work. It was starkly realised that this, together with the events of 9/11 and 7/7, highlighted the need for open discussion about difference, racial hatred and the need for cohesive thought and multiorganisational working (Sardar, 2005).

As in the 1985 Swann Report, the child was identified as a valuable resource and schools were encouraged to try and develop religious respect through dialogue with a variety of cultural groups. Local Authorities began to establish youth SACREs – a forum for the pupil's voice to be heard and where children were encouraged to become more involved in the decision making process on what RE provision should be offered to them in the post-9/11 society. Some authorities, such as Lancashire, have succeeded in developing a very active group who meet on a regular basis and who held their first youth conference in 2007.

Since the new millennium, there has also been an influx of funding for educational programmes about religion, which has found its way into mainstream television and not been simply reserved for schools, colleges or university courses. Religious programmes such as *Am I Normal?*, *Sacred Music* (BBC, 2008), *Around the World in 80 Faiths* (BBC, 2009), *The Seven Wonders of the Muslim World* (Channel 4, 2008) and *Christianity: A History* (Channel 4, 2009) show that there has been a shift towards educating the general public through television programmes that are broadcast at peak viewing times and which use current filming trends such as a familiar and well-respected presenter or through a form of reality TV. This is obviously a product of 9/11 and the War on Terrorism and so, in the twenty-first century, religion (in particular Islam) seems to be a popular topic at home and in schools, and programmes such as these show that the Government and television networks are using Religious Education to raise awareness of religious and cultural similarities, difference, practice and belief in an effort to instil understanding and thus respect.

However, media coverage has still had its part to play in highlighting the flaws of religion and reflecting some of the changing values of what some consider to be a post-religious society (Anderson, 2005). The journalist, Sharmeen Obaid-Chinoy, presented a *Dispatches* programme about Islamic extremism and child terrorists in Pakistan in March 2009 (Channel 4, 16 March 2009); and June 2008 saw news coverage of the marriage of two homosexual priests in the Anglican Church, which caused a rift in the Church of England similar to that over the ordination of women in the 1990s. Some clergy, such as the Archbishop of Uganda, considered the blessing to be against traditional teachings, yet some liberalists accepted the blessing and felt it was more in tune with the changing attitudes of today's society. As for schools, such debates are now encouraged and incorporated within RE schemes of work, and issues related to Humanism are now identified as valid modules that should be studied within the realms of Religious Education in schools (Gledhill, 2008).

An overview of the history of RE

As we have briefly explored, when events happen, the values, experiences and attitudes of society change. Wars, mass media coverage of news stories, changing political regimes, immigration, new religious movements and modernisation have all had an impact on society and, consequently, an impact on Religious Education in schools. Because people can now move relatively freely and inexpensively around the world; experience different cultures and ways of thinking and live in more than one place within a lifetime, there is no one clearly accepted way of living. People have more choice in how to live their life than ever before and are able to demonstrate this in a variety of ways. However, this can adversely affect the status quo, resulting at times in conflict, fear and ultimately war.

Through media such as television and the Internet, however, society can now be educated into considering different choices, so that people no longer need to hold parochial viewpoints, but can and should widen their knowledge and reflections to take on board new approaches. They can also communicate through a variety of media to people who live 2000 miles away and realise that the society they live in is no longer local but global. Therefore, in today's multifaceted global society it is essential that Religious Education in schools should reflect a global responsibility to each other; we are not just living in a town in England but also the UK, Europe and the World; and in each region there will be similarities but also difference that needs to be acknowledged and accepted.

Summary of key points

The purpose of RE has evolved over decades and is influenced by society's attitudes. Its purpose now is to

- Encourage personal and collective reflection on different and new ways of thinking
- Use modernisation as a positive influence on pupils so that they are able to voice opinions and think about how people live in their global and local communities
- Provide opportunities for pupils to work through half-formed ideas and try to remove any prejudice that might be prevalent because of family, peer pressure or lack of experience
- Provide pupils with information about how people live and why they make the choices they do
- Educate pupils into seeing the locality they live in as a microcosm of the global community
- Give all pupils the chance to decide for themselves who they want to be, based on well-informed creative lesson content.

Chapter 3
The value of Religious Education

LEARNING OBJECTIVES

In this chapter we will consider:

- The value of a skills-based approach to RE
- Communication skills in RE
- Reflective skills in RE
- Thinking skills in RE
- Enquiry skills in RE

It will also address elements within the following Standards:

Q1, Q3, Q4, Q10, Q14, Q18, Q19, Q29

Introduction: What is the value of RE in primary schools?

As we have seen in Chapter 1, valuing something is subjective and so appreciating and understanding the worth of Religious Education depends on the various experiences that you have had and your personal perspectives. It is an unfortunate fact that negative experiences tend to occasion inhibitions, natural reserve and insecurities, which can inhibit opportunities that would otherwise allow further development (Dowling, 2000).

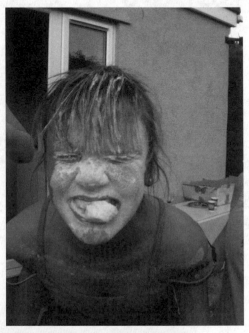

When we take time to observe children at play, it is obvious that they see a wonder and value in things that, as adults, we may no longer appreciate. Adults in a paddling pool may notice the coldness of the pipe whereas a child would marvel at the water pouring from it: they find worth in small experiences because they are naturally inquisitive (Abbott and Langston, 2005:155).

As illustrated by the influential social constructivist, Jerome Bruner, children naturally want to discover and experience their environment (Bruner, 1987) and so it is important that you encourage exploration of it. Teachers should not stifle children's search for meaning by using the captive audience to soapbox personal prejudices, perspectives or insecurities of RE. It is up to the children to make up their own minds about how to live and what to think and it is your responsibility within the RE lesson to provide opportunities for them to do just that. This is why RE is a valuable subject that can enhance the overall curriculum through developing the skills of enquiry, questioning and personal reflection.

The value of a skills-based approach to RE

Remnants of the indoctrinatory nature of RI before the 1988 Education Reform Act can still be felt today in the attitudes of some parents and even some teachers. From working with some of my trainees, I have realised that many people still seem to think that RE is not an academic subject, and that its value lies in moral education or instilling religious tolerance. Some parents still misunderstand the value of RE, so much so that they take advantage of 'the Conscience Clause' (see Chapter 2), which remains in current legislation, and remove their child from collective worship and RE lessons. However, RE is an excellent subject for developing Personal Learning and Thinking Skills, commonly referred to as PLTS (http://www.qca.org.uk/qca_13476.aspx), and Belle Wallace's (2001) concept of Thinking Actively in a Social Context (TASC), which will be explored in more depth in Chapter 10. The QCA has suggested PLTS should be a focus for 11–19 year olds, yet many of the six areas identified could apply to younger children, because they are the same skills that teachers are encouraged to explore within RE lessons, i.e. skills such as communication, reflection, thinking and enquiry.

The value of communication skills in RE

Good Religious Education lessons should allow children to reflect on what they have learnt through offering opportunities to discuss ideas. Yet to be able to discuss, a child needs to have some experience of emotional literacy to be able to explore what they mean and want to say. Ernst von Glasersfeld's research explored 'radical constructivism' and identified a connection between knowledge and language. He explored how experience, which he believes to be subjective, has an effect on the interpretation of knowledge and language (1995:1). It is difficult for a child to communicate what they know and understand because not everyone interprets knowledge and language in the same way. Consequently, translating such knowledge requires a good grasp of culturally accepted vocabulary and some sort of shared experience (1995:129). For example, my 3-year-old niece, Emily, was in church with her mother. As part of the Mass, the Roman Catholic priest and the congregation say, 'The Fruit of the Vine and work of human hands, it will become our spiritual drink.' Emily turned to my sister and asked enthusiastically, 'Are we having fruit and drink Mummy?' She was quite despondent when she realised that she was only to receive a blessing.

Case Study   Communicating knowledge

A small group of children were taking part in a series of lessons about Easter and were discussing the designs they had created that represented to them the Resurrection of Jesus and how they personally felt about it. The discussion about their designs opened up many issues about what they understood about Easter and Jesus. Below is an overview of their conversation:

'It's an airship that brings special people to life.'

And, when asked how it related to Jesus and to how he feels about the Resurrection, he shrugged.

This response demonstrated that B did not seem to have the emotional vocabulary to explain how his stone related to Jesus' Resurrection and to himself. C helped him explain the relationship by referring to her understanding of history and relating it to her stone and then to his. (The stone represents the stone that covered Jesus' tomb and which rolled away when he had risen.)

'[Mine] looks like a speech bubble – they didn't have computers to send messages they used speech instead. This is a message in a stone. Maybe B's spaceship is the same?'

C had begun to relate how the Resurrection was a message to Christians, but still didn't say how it related to her feelings, mainly due to having a limited emotional vocabulary. B looked puzzled by her reference to spaceships and then M referred to his own design and said,

'It's me and it's like the stone would have been sand colour in the tomb. It's me 'cause I'm Catholic, and I know Jesus was a Jew not a Catholic, but was one eventually.'

This response was insightful, as it showed that M was able to begin to articulate the link between the Resurrection of Jesus to himself as a Roman Catholic, yet his comments sparked a discussion which showed that the children had half-formed ideas and different understandings about Jesus and had some difficulty expressing them.

'Jesus wasn't a Jew!' (J almost shouting.)
'Yes he was! He was a Jew and he became a Catholic.' (M)
'But Jews killed him!' (J)
'No they didn't! (Pause) They didn't like him!' (C)
'Jesus wasn't a Jew, he's always been a Catholic.' (B)
'No he became Catholic when he died!' (M looking puzzled)
'I think M only wanted to do himself [on his stone] and didn't really think about Jesus.' (C)

The conversation ended here and moved on to a different topic, but M was sullen from then on.

This discussion supports von Glasersfeld's work, as many of the children lacked the language skills to articulate clearly what they were thinking, because the religious concepts were quite difficult to understand. They also didn't have agreed understandings that connected to common experiences between the children. The discussion also highlighted that J and M were astonished that they had different ideas about Jesus and hadn't realised until now.

Source: A county primary school, Lancashire

Because communication is a fundamental life skill, it needs to be practised, but to be able to do it well, children need to have common experiences so that they can understand their own and other' perspectives. Verbal communication has become an important method in RE for exploring and developing understanding of personal and cultural identity, yet there are many ways in which RE encourages communication that need not be written or verbal such as Art, Dance and Music, etc.

The *Non Statutory Framework* (QCA, 2004), alongside many schemes of work from Local Authorities and Diocese, incorporates a selection of communication tools to help children convey their understanding. The Catholic Truth Society (CTS) published *The Way, the Truth and the Life* series for Roman Catholic schools to follow (CTS, 2002). Most of the activities ask children to communicate their understanding through a written piece of work and frequently include aspects of Drama and Art (CTS, 2002:71). Likewise 'The Spiritual Education Project' examined by Andrew Wright (in Grimmit, 2000:170-87) considered how pupils developed their religious literacy through the pedagogy of critical Religious Education: communicating how the inner voice links with the outer reality or truth was fundamental to the project, as was how to express it in varying forms. Accordingly, communicating thought is a key life skill and one which RE is well equipped to develop since, by its innate nature, religious belief and practice isn't always verbal and is, at times, communicated in other physical and artistic forms.

Thus, your role in Religious Education lessons is to direct pupils towards communicating their innermost thoughts so as to make sense of the outer reality. Communication, whether verbal or not, is valuable in Religious Education lessons as it is the only tool that a child can use to publicly express their internal thoughts and help them create their own sense of self and identity, which is a key aim of RE (QCA, 2004:8).

The value of reflective skills in RE

To be reflective a child needs space, yet in today's busy schools it is difficult to gain any physical or emotional space to help mental clarity. Break times are noisy; classrooms are focused on producing an outcome and in between times are usually moments when the child is active in doing rather than taking time to ponder. RE, however, can be a forum that provides room for a child to consider issues that may be bothering them or an opportunity to voice simple thoughts that may seem insignificant, yet once aired are a chance to explore half-formed opinions and create mental space for a more focused understanding.

Reflection in RE advocates either a radical constructivist (Von Glasersfeld, 1995) or social constructivist (Vygotsky, 1978, cited in Daniels, 2001) mode of learning as it encourages discussion with others about personal understanding of the world. However, as explained earlier, to be able to communicate, children must first have common experiences, which then develop into personal opinions, and so it makes sense that children should be given time to think quietly before communicating what they believe to be reality. Although Cowley considers that a classroom which is noisy can confuse children (2004:74), I feel that some form of noise is necessary when teamwork and discussion is involved, because it's needed to develop Personal Learning and Thinking Skills (PLTS) and so quiet time can be used with noisy time. Within RE the value of having time to reflect will allow a child to form questions, which will in turn encourage clarity in what a child knows and understands before then investigating and discovering new answers within a team and communicating responses.

It is important to distinguish between thinking and reflecting, however, as reflecting can be seen as another word for thinking and it is easy to confuse the two. I would suggest that reflection is the method of slowing down the thinking process so that a child isn't an Activist immediately reacting to a question or opinion (Honey and Mumford, 1986), but first deliberates on what they know; considers what they understand and then ruminates on what they need to do next to help them discover more and learn from the original stimulus. Each stage encourages thinking, but is a stepping-stone within the process, hence the value of the skill of reflection in RE is that it allows children occasion and freedom to create more considered responses to events that happen within school and the wider global community.

The value of thinking skills in RE

To have an opinion, a child must have considered what they think, and usually this opinion is a result of discussions, interpreting data from the television or the Internet and generally reflecting on what they already know. It is part of the Piagetian process to developmental learning of Assimilation, Accommodation and Adaptation (Atkinson, 2006:15) and so to be able to form an opinion they need to create their own schemata and add a new idea or experience to pre-existing information, accommodate thinking so that they realise it is a new piece of information and then adapt the former opinion to create a new piece of understanding. For example, a child may have an idea that the Tooth Fairy is real because that has been their experience. They then discover by chance that their mum or dad, not Tinkerbell, removed the tooth and put a coin there instead, so they then need to acknowledge this new piece of information and consider it, so that they can come up with a logical reason for what they experienced. Much of this is an internal dialogue, yet often it is externalised through asking questions and discussing answers.

This is the general thinking process that everyone goes through and is also the learning and teaching pedagogy advocated throughout RE. In good Religious Education lessons, children are given opportunities to discuss what they already know about religions, themes or specific aspects of a religion through a variety of activities (assimilation). They are then asked to investigate what they have experienced and consider new information that they have discovered in order to debate any initial ideas that they may have (accommodation). Finally, they are encouraged to reflect on what they personally think of the new ideas and attitudes explored and formulate their newest informed opinion (adaptation).

Curriculum 2000 states that children should be encouraged to think rationally and creatively, because the skill of thinking is considered an important tool and will not be improved upon if there are no opportunities for it to be practised (QCA, 1999:22). The *Non Statutory Framework for RE* suggests that thinking is a fundamental part of the learning and teaching of RE (QCA, 2004:16, 18), and questions such as 'Who am I?', 'Where do I belong?', 'What happens when someone dies?' are suggested starting points for activities within many schemes of work. Even very young children are encouraged and able to ask such questions and begin to think about them through asking 'Big and Little' questions (http://www.teachers.tv/video/2836). Thus, developing the skill of thinking involves confidence, reasoning, memory, logic and creativity, all approaches that will be useful in future careers (Cowley, 2004:3). Consequently, thinking skills acquired through RE are valuable in preparing children for life.

The value of enquiry skills in RE

The pedagogy of enquiry is about children discovering for themselves what they want to know and how they want to learn. Personalised learning is another way of looking at it and is an approach which the Department for Children Schools and Families (DfCSF) is pleased to see in schools (http://www.standards.dfes.gov.uk/personalisedlearning/about/). As all children have differing needs and learning challenges, it is important that schools support the natural curiosity of learning, hence providing the children with an education system that encourages enquiry-based learning. RE can do just that!

Enquiry in RE is investigation into a question and the process of finding out answers. This will then lead to more questions, which in turn lead to more examination and analysis of what has been discovered. It can be taught through challenges such as a statement where the children prove or disprove it through debate, discussion, research, etc. or it can be through clearly designed activities that scaffold the children to one answer or religious 'truth', which in turn inspires further learning and questions. Within enquiry-based learning, it will be the children who form the *why* and *what* of the learning process and you, the teacher, who directs and shapes it towards the *how, when* and *so what?* This process of active enquiry-based thinking is advocated in RE syllabi such as the Lancashire Agreed Syllabus and is called the 'Field of Enquiry' approach that originated from the 1960s Westhill project (Brown and Broadbent, 2002).

Being able to consider and ask difficult questions that may not have a set answer is a skill that promotes independent thought and confidence. Enquiring into why something happens, how people live and what people believe, without being too hung up on not being able to come to one clearly agreed conclusion, is fundamental to personal growth, as it allows a child to respect their peer's differing opinion without hatred or indifference. This skill should be practised in the Religious Education classroom and will, in the current climate of religious extremism and the possibility of climate refugees in the near future, be essential for the next generation. As the framework states, 'Religious education has an important role in preparing pupils for adult life, employment and lifelong learning' (QCA, 2004:9).

Summary of key points

The value of Religious Education is to

- Help children develop life long skills
- Offer opportunities to improve skills in discussion, reflection, communication, thinking and questioning
- Encourage children to develop a unique identity yet principally, RE allows them to explore who they want to be by evaluating what they think, feel and believe
- Have the opportunity to discuss, analyse and reflect on half-formed ideas within a safe environment
- Give children the space they need to consider what they really think about certain life choices, so that any choice they make in the future can be an informed one that is compatible with their personalities and convictions
- Nurture respect not tolerance. Respect for themselves as people with valid ideas; respect for others who are brave enough to think and live differently and respect for the local and global society in which they live

The value of RE is immense and through creative RE lessons children can become confident, imaginative, individualistic, reflective, respectful team-workers who can make an important difference in this world. The following chapters will explore how you can exploit the potential value of various pedagogies and approaches in RE.

Chapter 4
Creatively connecting RE

LEARNING OBJECTIVES

In this chapter we will consider:

- The difference between cross-curricular and thematic learning
- How Religious Education connects with the creative and expressive arts
- The brief history of the creative and expressive arts within Religion

It will also address elements within the following Standards:

Q3, Q8, Q10, Q14, Q15, Q17, Q18, Q19, Q23, Q25

Introduction

Although RE works well with all the subjects of the National Curriculum, this and the following four chapters will explore Religious Education with and through a specific focus of the curriculum, namely the creative and expressive arts. It is my intention to give you a flavour of how you can creatively connect RE to a specific curriculum area so that you can reflect on the examples provided and consider how to further develop the suggested activities and possibly translate them so that they can become suitable for other subjects such as Mathematics, Science, Geography or History, etc.

Creative approaches to RE

As we have already noted in Chapter 3, RE is a subject that lends itself well to developing PLTS (Personal Learning and Thinking Skills) and Personal Capabilities through Thinking Actively in a Social Context: TASC (Wallace, 2001). As such, its value is in learning and improving skills that will be used throughout a person's life. Learning is an ongoing process and learning theory shows that children and adults learn mainly through experience of the environment they live in (Donaldson, 1987; Slee and Shute, 2003). It would seem logical, therefore, to combine the curriculum subjects into a more holistic practice, so that the children can make purposeful meaning of what they are required to learn. This certainly links with the recommendations of Jim Rose's interim review of the primary curriculum, in which he suggests areas of learning rather than individual subjects (BBC News, 8 December 2008; Rose, 2008).

Life and human experience are not divided into simple objectives. They are naturally holistic and a mishmash of learning events that are cross-curricular. Switching off my alarm at 6a.m., I shower, dress, clean my teeth, make breakfast, walk my dog, etc. These experiences are neither subject-specific nor divided into specialist subject areas. Similarly, children's everyday life experiences are not subject-specific. They do not think of Mathematics when setting alarms or Science when cleaning molars or PE when walking dogs. Such experiences are holistic and this is one of the arguments that educationalists offer for the curriculum to be thematic and skills-based, not subject-specific or objective-led (Bell, 1991; Stern, 2006).

Religious Education blends well with other subjects because it is innately about how people live, learn and think. Enquiry, reflection, thinking and communication are skills that are not only evident in RE, but also in other curriculum subjects. Hence, RE can be taught simultaneously with other subjects because, although they may have different objectives, they develop the same Key Skill (Watson and Thompson, 2007). It seems ironic, however, that Religious Education remains outside the National Curriculum, even though it could be argued that it is the only subject out of the nine that naturally blends well with the others (see Chapter 2 for the purpose of RE).

Connecting in a cross-curricular or thematic way

It is important, however, to make a distinction between cross-curricular and thematic styles of teaching. It is very easy to confuse the two, as they seem to do the same thing. However, there is a subtle difference. Cross-curricular teaching and learning is where two subjects are taught simultaneously. For example the objective of observational drawing in Art (National Curriculum KS2 1a, 5a, 5d) is taught at the same time as the objective of the features of a place of worship in RE (Non Statutory Framework KS2 AT1b, 3g). Both objectives are taught in tandem, i.e. how to draw a specific detail within the architectural feature of a font alongside its religious and doctrinal purpose. Jonathan Barnes (2007) makes a similar distinction that cross-curricular teaching should be skills or curriculum focused and that usually only two, and in some cases three, subjects are taught simultaneously, because teaching the objectives of four or more subjects to a satisfactory, if not good, level can become too difficult to manage and assess.

Thematic teaching, however, is where three or more subjects can be taught with similar themes, yet the objectives of only one of the subjects will be developed and taught within the lesson. For example, 'Our locality' is a familiar theme in many Geography syllabi (QCA Unit 6) and would link well with RE and a visit to a place of worship such as a mosque. Such a visit would not require the children to undertake a local study and so they would not be taught a specific geographical skill, but would look at how faith is expressed within a religious building. The teacher touches on the theme of locality because the religious building is within the local geography of the school but does not teach it directly whilst at the mosque.

It is possible to teach an RE lesson through either method; both work well, yet it is important that you don't assume that you are teaching in a cross-curricular way purely because there is a link with another subject. Unless you are teaching and assessing the objectives of two subjects within one lesson, you are teaching thematically.

Remember that:

- Cross-curricular teaching is planning and teaching specific learning objectives for at least two subjects simultaneously.
- Thematic teaching is teaching RE within a theme that links to other subjects.

We will explore how to organise and plan for creative RE in Chapter 10.

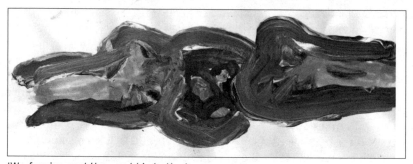

'We forgive and the world is better'

'We forgive each other'

Historical connections: religion and the Arts

There are many academic texts that discuss how Art, Dance and Music have always been used as a form of worship in religion yet, looking at sacred texts and the images within religious icons (i.e., stained glass windows, paintings, sculpture, artefacts used within the religion such as a chalice or offertory plate), you can also see that Dance and Music have been a form of religious expression for centuries.

Traditional religions such as Aboriginal, African, Egyptian and Greek show dance and musical objects in their oldest art forms and are used within their religious rituals. Many authors such as Wosien (1992) believe that man's divine relationship with God is shown through dance and this is depicted in early art. The Acts of St John, Ecclesiastes, Psalms (Ps150) and the Upanishads support this idea as each mention the expressive arts in some way. Dance and Music are seen as expressions of man's relationship with the gods and his understanding of the world in which he lives; it is his way of interpreting what he thinks and feels.

Religious art is a useful tool in exploring how the other art forms are used in religion. There are a variety of images that relate to Dance and Music in a selection of faith traditions, although Hinduism may possibly be the most illustrative: many Hindu gods are seen dancing and playing musical instruments. For example, Krishna (an avatar of Vishnu) is considered a great musician and Shiva Nataraja, who is occasionally called 'Lord of the Dance', is often shown dancing a five-part dance that represents Creation, Veiling, Preservation, Destruction and Release within a circle of fire (Blurton, 1994). The Hindu goddess of knowledge, music and the arts, Saraswati, is also occasionally seen holding a sitar or other musical instrument.

The ancient world regarded music as one of the most potent forms of magic and power. One of the Hindu creation stories shows that the world started with the sound of Om (sometimes written as Aum), which resonated throughout the universe and woke Vishnu, who was curled asleep inside the coils of a snake, and began the Earth through directing Brahma to create the various elements within it. In this Hindu tradition it seems that music began creation.

In the new millennium, Art, Dance and Music are still important factors and are frequently used in the weekly and daily acts of worship in a variety of faith traditions. They are also used during rites of passage ceremonies such as funerals, weddings, births and initiation ceremonies; indeed, music was used throughout the inauguration of the first African American President Barak Obama on 20 January 2009. The creative and expressive arts, therefore, seem to be a logical starting point for teaching the Key Skills of Religious Education and connecting them to the objectives of a National Curriculum subject.

How to make connections

Reflecting on how Art, Dance, Drama and Music are used within various religions it is noticeable that they can be categorised into three distinct purposes; namely they can be used for religious worship; as a mode of religious expression and as a method for establishing the connection with a divine presence through the spirit being uplifted.

Religious worship

Worship is the nuts and bolts of any religion, and understanding that people express their faith in different ways is the first step to respecting and valuing the difference and similarities between the faiths. It is important that children are aware of the various ways people worship a God or gods in their faith, so that they don't develop stereotypical views. Not every religious denomination has a regular religious service or a set format or structure within it; some faith traditions use a variety of techniques that are different from the stereotypical image of worship. Many use an amalgam of approaches, thus making the religion fresh and contemporary as is explored in the BBC 2 televisions programme and resulting book *Around the World in 80 Faiths* (Owen-Jones, 2009). Looking at Art, Dance, Drama and Music is the first step to considering why people worship and links nicely to Attainment Target 1 (Learning About Religion) in the *Non Statutory Framework for RE* (QCA, 2004:34).

Religious expression

How the religion is expressed is similar to worship, as worship is a form of religious expression, yet what I mean here is how a religious person expresses their feelings and opinions about their faith. Expression can be personal through an individualistic form of Art, Dance, Drama or Music or through an organised or set piece of music or dance that someone else has created and the religious person interprets. Either way the religious person's identity and personal reflections can be explored through each mode and help them discover how they truly feel about their faith. Exploring religious expression with children can help them begin to consider what they personally feel about a given concept (religious or not) and creatively show their ideas through the creative and expressive arts.

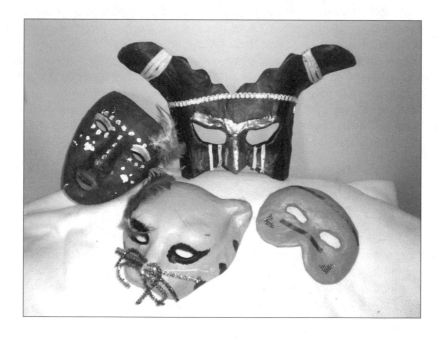

Spiritual uplifting

Not everyone believes in a spirit; however, in traditional faith traditions the spirit or soul is an important element to religious expression and worship. Yet, whether a child believes in a soul or not, they can identify in some way with extreme human emotions such as feeling elated, happy, sad and depressed (Euade, 2008:13–28). Many religions use the creative and expressive arts as a way to connect their soul to a divine presence and feel their soul uplifted. They utilise the arts to help make the relationship with God or gods closer.

Exploring this idea with children may help them consider why they feel sad or happy, and become more aware of what they need to do to understand this emotion so that they can grow on a personal level. Thus, the purpose of spiritual uplifting in this case and RE in general is not for them to develop a closer relationship with a God or gods, but for them to develop a closer relationship with themselves (ibid.). Knowing who they are and what they think can be the first step a child takes to intra-personal intelligence (Gardner, 1993), and this can then lead to a developed self-concept and ultimately personal happiness. Chapters 2 and 3 explore this concept in more depth, while Robert Coles' (1990) text, which further explores children's spirituality, is well worth reading.

Summary of key points

Understanding how religions use the creative and expressive arts as a way to interpret personal faith can help you make connections between Art, Dance, Drama and Music and the Key Skills of RE. Such connections can become an excellent way of developing Attainment Target 2 (Learning From Religion) within the *Non Statutory Framework* (QCA, 2004) and help you improve your skills as a creative teacher. Remember:

- There is a slight difference between cross-curricular and thematic teaching
- Art, Dance, Drama and Music have always had a strong connection to religion
- The creative and expressive arts are a way for man to have a close relationship with a God or gods
- Religions use the creative and expressive arts as a
  - Form of worship
  - Form of expression
  - A way to lift the spirit

Chapters 5, 6, 7 and 8 will explore how to integrate Art, Dance, Drama and Music with RE and will suggest a selection of activity ideas on which you can reflect and then adapt to suit the classes you teach.

Chapter 5
What are the connections between Art and RE?

LEARNING OBJECTIVES

In this chapter we will consider:

- Creative use of Art to enhance Religious Education

It will also address elements within the following Standards:

Q3, Q8, Q10, Q14, Q15, Q17, Q18, Q19, Q23, Q25

Introduction

This chapter is written to help you consider how you can creatively connect with and through the Art curriculum. It includes some real case studies of schools and teachers I have worked with and a small selection of activity ideas.

RE and visual art

Over the years I have asked trainee teachers and children to look at and reflect on religious art. Responses have been frustration, inspiration, confusion and in some cases, outrage, especially when we have looked at and discussed the use of religious imagery in advertising. This is why I see art as a fantastic vehicle for learning about (Attainment Target 1) and learning from (Attainment Target 2) religion (QCA, 2004:34).

Religion and art have formed a strong bond over the centuries because, like text, art is a sophisticated way of communicating a religious message (Jensen, 2000:3). Historically, religious leaders have promoted doctrine to the congregation and extended the traditional messages of the religion mainly through the use of oral tradition, because society wasn't literate, yet art in religious buildings (and eventually in Psalters and scrolls, etc.) has been another method of putting the message across (Gouldberg, 2004:176).

Religious messages can be seen in the earliest art forms, for example, in early Byzantine icons that show narratives of Biblical stories (Nes, 2006) and Buddhist art depicting the Buddha's enlightenment such as the 1500-year-old *Bamiyan* statues of Afghanistan that were bombed in March 2001 by the Taliban. In later periods, however, the conventional use of symbols in religious art (iconography) and the meaning of these symbols seemed to be more widely understood and acknowledged by the general population, who were able to read the visual language within them. Religious paintings and sculptures presented the fundamental principles of the faith so that an illiterate member of the congregation could learn from them, so both were necessary for learning about the religion (Jensen, 2000:3).

The iconography within religious art highlighted the most important elements of the Gospel (Nes, 2006); for example in a Crucifixion painting Jesus would be placed in the middle to show his central importance to the story and religion. Similarly, Mary, who is seen by Christians as the Mother of God and Queen of Heaven, would be painted in blue or purple representing royalty and heaven's colour. Occasionally, symbols in the art would be a lily to show purity/chastity; a halo implying the person is holy or a dove to remind Christians of the gifts of the Holy Spirit (Davis, 2005). Such messages are seen within oil paintings and triptychs. However, possibly the most common form of art available to the masses historically and today would be within stained glass windows that were built into the structures of the sacred space and which also contained iconographic motifs.

However, iconography was and is not only reserved for Christianity. Whereas Islam includes pattern and calligraphy as an art form, showing the spiritual aspects of objects and beings (www.bbc.co.uk/religion/religions/islam/art), Hinduism uses colourful paintings and statues as part of their daily worship and each god holds items that are an emblem for their characteristics. Whatever the religion, each piece of art or icon that has been produced is likely to contain a message about the fundamental belief systems of the faith and how to practise it. Traditionally, the purpose was to reinforce and teach the doctrine of the faith (Nes, 2006:13).

In the twenty-first century, the majority of society are able to read and write, so there has not been such a need to retell and teach religious doctrine in art and probably as a result, most of the general understanding of iconography has been lost to the populace. Consequently, today's art serves a different purpose, as it seems to be more in tune with the expression of an artist's faith and/or interpretation of the religious story.

The late Liverpool artist, Arthur Dooley (www.arthurdooley.co.uk), created a vast amount of religious art. He has a selection of amazing sculpture housed in and on religious buildings throughout Liverpool such as in the Scandinavian Church, in the Anglican Cathedral and on the side of a Methodist Church in Toxteth. He has created art that has a strong personal message that is both religious and political; including his response to the Holocaust and religion in general. As part of the City of Culture, there is a fantastic opportunity to conduct a walking tour around Liverpool to see his art and reflect on the messages within them (www.liverpoolmusuems.co.uk/dooley/christ01.html).

There are also wonderful examples of early and modern Christian religious art in the Sainsbury Wing of the National Gallery in London (www.nationalgallery.org.uk). Also in London, The Victoria and Albert Museum (www.vam.ac.uk) houses huge religious sculpture from various places around the world. However, other museums such as the World Museum in Liverpool (www.liverpoolmuseums.org.uk/wml) and The Barber Institute of Arts (www.barber.org.uk) in Birmingham also have religious art exhibited and are worth a look. Most museums and galleries have excellent education departments, so arranging a visit with one would be a good learning experience for your class as some provide bespoke workshops that can help you explore specific RE objectives.

Connecting with the Art curriculum

The Art and Design curriculum identifies how pupils should explore art in order to develop their own ideas. Generally, they are expected to ask questions about their work and the work of others; reflecting on them in order to consider what they think and feel (QCA, 1999:118–21). Such requirements are also Key Skills in Religious Education and because, according to Miller (2003:204) imagination is essential for good Art and good RE as it encourages critical thinking, it seems obvious to me that Art and RE are perfectly matched.

Connecting RE with Art can help children begin to consider what they think and feel about how artists have addressed puzzling questions, while also helping them to respond to the big issues in their own lives, thus enabling them to achieve AT2 (Learning from Religion). Below are a few examples with case studies on how to develop Personal Learning and Thinking Skills (PLTS) through cross-curricular or thematic RE and Art.

Exploring with RE and Art

As was discussed in Chapter 4, cross-curricular learning involves simultaneously teaching the objectives of two or more subjects. It is, therefore, important that when creating an Art and RE activity, you ensure you are teaching the objectives of both subjects and not simply focusing on Religious Education, otherwise you could be in danger of teaching neither well (Miller, 2003:209). That means you need to consider teaching the concepts of colour pattern, texture, tone, form, line, etc., and the skills of printing, collage, pastels, paints, sketching, etc., alongside the Personal Learning and Thinking skills of communication, reflection, thinking and enquiry that are required within a good RE lesson (see Chapter 3).

Emotional literacy

Like Dance, Drama and Music, Art is used in religion as a means for spiritual expression, interpretation and uplifting yet, for a child to be able to communicate what they feel, they first need the vocabulary to be able to express themselves. Explaining feelings can be a difficult concept for those who have a good grasp of language, and for a child who is constantly learning new vocabulary it can seem even more daunting, as they are trying to understand what certain words mean to them (Donaldson, 1987). Art, therefore, can be a medium that encourages a child first to reflect on how they feel and then create something that they can discuss and evaluate, thus supporting them with acquiring emotional language. Try to use Art in RE lessons as a way to help the child to internally analyse their personal thoughts and reflections about what religion and being religious means to them. The Art in Religious Education should be the outcome of a personal journey that has enabled a child to develop a sense of self, and it should not be subjected to public appraisal.

Case Study   **Communicating knowledge**

Action research in a Roman Catholic (RC) primary school, Lancashire
Pentecost and Easter – exploring personal religious identity and the use of emotional language.

As part of the RC *The Way, the Truth and the Life* scheme of work (CTS, 2002), the children were required to learn about the Easter story. The objective of the scheme was to understand how the coming of the Holy Spirit at Pentecost changed the disciples, but the activity was adapted from the scheme to create an art-based learning experience. The class had explored the concept of choice and forgiveness in previous lessons and this session was the penultimate lesson for the run up to Easter.

The children reflected on what they had already explored about Jesus' resurrection and then took part in a retelling of the Pentecostal story. They were asked to consider in talk partners how they thought the disciples felt before and after they were filled with the Holy Spirit. This required empathy and a good use of descriptive language to be able to explain emotions. The general class feedback showed that they used a limited vocabulary such as happy, excited and overjoyed, which seemed to touch on the feelings that the RC Church wanted the children to understand, but did not necessarily develop their religious awareness of how the story related to them as Roman Catholics. To be able to do this the children needed to relate the story of the disciples receiving the Holy Spirit to themselves and this was a very difficult and mature concept to grasp.

The art activity therefore tried to bridge this as it asked the children to make a cone that represented them. The cone was plain on the outside but the children were asked to change the inside in a way that visually represented how they or the disciples felt after being blessed by the Holy Spirit. They could use pastels and design it in anyway they wished. So that the children could explore the materials independently and not feel that there was a 'right' way of presenting their art, a ready-made example was not provided.

On an artistic note, the children were familiar with pastels, yet when a teaching moment was noticed, the children were encouraged to colour mix and smudge the pastels to produce different textures. It was intended that the children developed the Art Programme of Study 2 a&b which was to investigate and explore the visual and tactile qualities of pastels and develop their control of the medium and so this lesson was cross-curricular Art and RE.

The visual outcome was more interesting than the verbal feedback as the children's art was more expressive and the language they used to explain it was varied. Some chose to draw themselves or an object whereas others chose to use colours and no specific form to express how they felt when blessed by the Holy Spirit. Some children explained that they felt "squirly" and "filled up with colour" which seemed more emotionally descriptive than the previous "happy".

All children used bright colours and suggested that this was because they were cheerful colours and the Holy Spirit made them feel 'floaty' and uplifted. However, some children drew pictures that did not relate to the objective thus showing that they were still developing their ideas and understanding of religious identity. This activity enabled the children to develop their personal religious journey at their own rate without feeling there was a right or wrong answer and consider what, if anything, the Holy Spirit meant personally to them.

Source: Adapted from Chamberlain and Northcott, 2009

Other methods to develop emotional literacy and personal understanding of a religious event or doctrine could be to create a visual metaphor for a concept such as *pilgrimage, resurrection, love* or *wealth*. The children could use a variety of styles to draw, create a sculpture, use clay, make a collage or use any other artistic device to represent what they think the terminology or concept meant to them. This can be undertaken on an individual or group basis and would encourage them to discuss their ideas, thus enabling them to clarify their opinions. It would also allow them to refine their artistic capabilities alongside their religious vocabulary.

Architecture

Religious buildings seem to have had considerable thought and energy put into their creation. It is fascinating to see the type of buildings and the styles associated with particular religions, such as minarets and mosaics on mosques, domes and turrets on eastern orthodox churches and gargoyles on cathedrals, etc. Each facet and design feature serves a distinct purpose and can relate to the belief systems of that faith or society of the time.

It is also interesting to notice the stylistic features of architecture during certain periods in history, e.g. Victorian compared to a 1970s building, or even compare how history has affected a religious building and its architecture over the years. The Anglican Cathedral in Liverpool is a fine example of this, having many different styles in one building as it took 74 years to complete.

There is some fantastic religious architecture in the UK that is worth exploring through a walking tour focusing on the differences and similarities of buildings in a locality and the purpose of sacred space, i.e., for worship, but also for community links and to help build a sense of belonging. In fact, walking around a small area of Preston called *Ashton in Ribble* in 2009, I noticed five different Christian churches within a square mile and each had different stylistic features due to their age or religious denomination. This isn't an unusual phenomenon.

Alternatively there are websites that virtually explore religious buildings. http://www.stumbleupon.com/s/#1jp8LY/villageofjoy.com/20-usual-churches-parti//topic:Architecture hosts amazing images of 20 unusual churches around the world ranging from fantastical to awe-inspiring. Each church has chosen its location and design for a particular reason and would be a great stimulus for children to begin to see the purpose of a place of worship and what the design features represent. They could then (after receiving a brief) design and create their own religious building using a selection of suitable materials that match the language, artistic and religious skills of their age. Eventually they would present their design and model to the 'client' (KS1 and 2 Programme of Study for Art 5 a&b).

Advertising

Advertisements are a complicated and potentially tricky concept to use with children because they need to have a good grasp of language and be able to consider somebody else's viewpoint to be able to debate the issues that the adverts raise. I would suggest using adverts with upper Key Stage 2 and KS3/4 for debate about how to be religiously sensitive; the influence of the media on religion and discussion on whether adverts promote tolerance or respect of religions. This would be thematic RE and Art rather than cross-curricular.

There are some interesting adverts that have used religious imagery to sell products, such as Nike's image of Wayne Rooney during the world cup with a red cross on his chest representing the St George flag, which is also a reference to the Crusades. This advert was in most sport retail outlets and it offended some people, as they felt it likened him to a saviour and placed him on an equal footing with Christ (Google images Wayne Rooney). Also PlayStation used an image of a man wearing a crown that were the symbols of PlayStation but looked like thorns, thus relating the image and the product to Christ's crucifixion (http://www.adverblog.com/archives/2005_09.htm). Another controversial issue is whether a secular image should be used to put across a religious message. The image and logo of the food-chain Kentucky Fried Chicken (KFC) has been adapted by American church groups to become a parody for a Youth for Christ project (YFC) and also a poster campaign to Keep Following Christ (Google images search engine). Some Humanists believe this to be in bad taste.

A good question to debate with children would be to discuss whether these images, or any religiously explicit image, should be used to sell a product. I advise, however, to use such an activity only when you know your class and parents very well and are able sensitively to discuss issues about religious tolerance without causing offence. The children could create a sketchbook and/or montage of their ideas about advertising and how it can affect how people feel about religion and society in general, which thematically links to the Art Curriculum (KS2 1a, 1c, 3a, 5a, 5d) and could eventually develop into a specific piece of distinctive art.

Looking at the imagery and symbols within an advert is fascinating and helps children understand that art is wider than a picture or sculpture. Everyday, the media (adverts, television, newspapers) can be a very powerful tool to turn someone onto or against religion (Badr, 2004). Consequently, they should be viewed and interpreted with caution because of the possibility of prejudice and/or questionable agendas when the items were created.

National Curriculum and Non Statutory Framework links

RE =	KS1	AT1 1c, 1d, 1e
		AT2 2a, 2b,
		Breadth of study 3g, 3j, 3o, 3p
	KS2	AT1 1b, 1c, 1d, 1e, 1g, 1h
		AT2 2a, 2b, 2c, 2d
		Breadth of study 3i, 3m, 3o, 3p, 3q, 3r
Art =	KS1	1a, 1b, 2a, 2b, 3a, 4a, 4c
	KS2	1a, 1b, 1c, 2a, 2b, 3a, 4a, 4b, 4c
	KS1 & 2	Breadth of study 5a, 5b, 5d

Interpretation of religion through visual art

There are many different ways visual artists explore their ideas about the world. They enjoy experimenting with a selection of styles and mediums such as paint, pastels, clay, line drawings, etc. to help them with their personal journey in making sense of the world. Children can learn from such a process within RE lessons and use it to explore some difficult concepts related to religion such as the Holocaust. Below are a few examples on how you can use visual art with either your KS1 or 2 class.

Cartoons

A graphic novel is a selection of cartoons that have a common theme or are about a certain character, e.g. Batman. The manuscripts that are usually produced as weekly or monthly supplements are collected together into a bound book and this book becomes a selection of short stories that, when read in sequence, develop into a novel. Different designs are used within graphic novels and these depend on the style of the artist, yet a very popular style is called 'Manga', which usually takes up a large section in most good bookshops.

A graphic novel is a fantastic genre to explore with children, especially as many schemes of work suggest producing a storyboard as an activity and this is often a KS1 activity. However, most schemes do not seem to suggest exploring the artistic element within the storyboard, so recreating the stylistic and artistic features of a graphic novel alongside an RE objective is an excellent way of teaching in a creative, cross-curricular way. There are two amazing graphic novels that I have come across, which would be fantastic to use with children. The first is *The Complete Maus* (more suitable for KS2), which is an amazing account of an Auschwitz survivor written by his son Art Spiegelman, and the second is *The Manga Bible* (Old and New Testaments) by Siku (www.themangabible.com) (suitable for KS1 and 2) that retells (using the Manga style) significant accounts within the Bible.

Case Study   **A Christmas graphic novel (3 lessons)**

Part-time second year trainee teacher Tracey Brooks was asked to teach the RE element of a scheme of work with a Key Stage 2 class. As it was nearing Christmas, the scheme required her to discuss the Christian Christmas story, but she was concerned that by Year 5 they had explored the story in lots of ways and she wanted to develop a more creative teaching approach.

Using *The Manga Bible: NT Extreme*, she looked at the events leading up to Jesus' birth and how his early life was portrayed. Tracey began by looking at how the artists chose to explore the event, discussing with the children the choice of dialogue, the stylistic features chosen by the artists for the people, the colours and use of shading and layout of the page, etc. She then talked about the importance of the events within the story and why the children thought the artists chose to highlight some aspects but not others. Finally, Tracey explained the religious message that the artists wanted to express and detailed how this art was their interpretation of the story and the faith.

The children were then placed in friendship groups and asked to produce their own version of the Christmas story. They were asked to try to replicate the Manga style or try to use some of its features. They were also encouraged to focus on how they wanted to interpret the story and what they wanted to show to the reader, e.g., rather than give a blow by blow account of the events they were encouraged to focus on the messages the story tries to share with Christians.

The outcome was amazing because the children learnt *about* the important elements of the Christmas story, but also learnt *from* it, as they focused on the Christian message and what it meant to them. Each piece of art was individuallstlc and was a personal interpretation of the story. The art demonstrated how the children chose to be creative through producing a style that was unique to them, yet using some of the Manga features, and presenting what they thought was important to the faith rather than what the teacher considered significant. Tracey was very pleased with the results and felt she had been more creative in producing a storyboard with a twist.

Although this is a KS2 example, the graphic novel idea has been used successfully with KS1 pupils, so it works equally well throughout the primary range.

Source: Year 5/6 pupils, Ribbleton Primary School, Lancashire

Windows

Most christian religious buildings have stained glass windows within them that present the message of the faith. However, in more recent times, stained glass windows have become a vehicle for the artist's interpretation of the messages of the faith (Archur, 2005).

Making a glass panel with children is expensive and dangerous, but there are some fantastic glass artists who can be employed to work with small groups of children. The World of Glass Museum in St Helens (www.worldofglass.com) offers workshops that can explore the glass process with classes. However, if you wanted to develop the concept of stained glass with very young children they could make a design template of a window out of thick black cardboard and then pour melted sugar that has been dyed into the gaps. As this is still quite dangerous, however, an alternate method could be to place different coloured boiled sweets into the gaps and then place the template and sweets in an oven for them to melt. Let them cool and then once varnished hang them in front of a window.

This thematic activity is mainly learning *about* religion and has some artistic value, but it is important to try and develop learning *from* religion in lessons, so the following case study should give you some ideas. I do advise, however, that you should reflect on how you could use this university example and adapt it for KS1 and 2.

Case Study   **Creating a stained glass window**

As part of the Year 2 RE element of the BA honours with QTS degree at Edge Hill University, trainee teachers are asked to consider the value of Religious Education and Art and explore how to teach it in a cross-curricular or thematic way. Each class was asked to produce a panel in small groups that was about a theme or a religious story. The panels were then collected together and stuck (using insulation and duct tape) onto a window to create a large display that showed the trainees' interpretations of the theme.

Cellophane windows

Three classes with approximately 25 trainees in each class looked at the theme Light Festivals and explored the stories of Diwali and Christmas. They researched the events, the themes and the messages within the stories and then as a small group designed a panel, which interpreted what they had learnt. They were given a blank template that was the size of the panel for their design (so that when all panels were put together the display wouldn't be too large for the window) and cut different colours of cellophane to fit their design. Occasionally, they experimented with colour mixing by placing different coloured cellophanes on top of each other. They were shown how to use insulation tape to stick two pieces of cellophane together so that the result was similar to the traditional stained glass window. The artistic skills that were practised were composition, manipulation of materials and collage (NC 1b, 2a, 2b, 2c, 4b, 5b, 5d).

Laminate windows

Eight other groups were given a theme such as Soul, Festival or Light. They were asked to reflect on what these words/themes meant to them and design a panel using a laminating pouch that showed their interpretation. The trainees were given an A3 or A4 laminate pouch and had access to various colours of cellophane that they would place inside the pouch to create a design. They were permitted to use colour printers, acetate pens and photographs as occasionally modern glass artists use writing, letters, photographs and other items in their work. It was interesting to see who chose to use words and photographs and who did not.

Most trainees glued their cellophane down on the inside of the pouch before using the heater to melt the sides together so that the design would stay in place during the final process.

The outcome was tremendous and although each group interpreted their theme differently, when each panel was placed together the window looked harmonious. It is interesting to see that the cellophane windows, which seemed more complicated to make, produced art that looked more traditional and seemed to be more in keeping with helping a trainee explore AT1, whereas the artistic methods for the laminate windows involved more personal expression and so was good for assessing AT2. The trainees loved seeing their art displayed in the front entrance of the Faculty and it has reminded me that no matter what age, we all like to have our work valued.

Source: Year 2 trainee teachers, Edge Hill University

Key Stage 1

I have used the laminate activity both with Year 1 children based on the Diwali story and with Year 5 children and it has been completed equally well. I noticed, however, that the children had difficulty with the skill of cutting cellophane and the creation of the initial design. Cutting is quite a tricky skill and cellophane is a difficult material to manage (when they rush or the design is too small, the cellophane ripped and the child became upset) so I suggest you provide lots of time for your class to make mistakes and take care when cutting.

As for the design, the children tended to make it too detailed and did not use their image as a design template, hence when they cut up the cellophane they either made mistakes because the design was too small or found that they couldn't remember which coloured piece belonged to which part of the design and became confused. It is best that you encourage your class to cut one piece at a time and either attach it to another piece using the tape or lightly glue it into the laminate (depending on which approach you take).

National Curriculum and Non Statutory Framework links

RE =	KS1	AT1 1c, 1d, 1e
		AT2 2a, 2b,
		Breadth of Study 3g, 3j, 3o, 3p
	KS2	AT1 1b, 1c, 1d, 1e, 1g, 1h
		AT2 2a, 2b, 2c, 2d
		Breadth of study 3i, 3m, 3o, 3p, 3q, 3r
Art =	KS1	1a, 1b, 2a, 2b, 3a, 4a, 4c
	KS2	1a, 1b, 1c, 2a, 2b, 3a, 4a, 4b, 4c
	KS1 & 2	Breadth of study 5a, 5b, 5d

Expression of religion through visual art

Interpretation and expression of religion are closely linked to the creative arts because the art is commonly created as a way to express an aspect of a person's faith. It is interesting to explore such art with children as they can then consider how they use art to express or help interpret how they feel.

Celebrations

Celebrations seem to be a common theme in RE schemes of work and so many schools like to look at what happens during festivals and how that festival is expressed. This is when thematic and cross-curricular art can support RE. For example, masks are frequently used in celebrations such as for dance (see Chapter 6) and in celebrations such as the Jewish festival of Purim. Likewise, during Diwali the community enjoy making Rangoli patterns on their doorsteps using coloured paints, dyes or seeds and light diva lamps, which are brightly painted clay thumb pots that are glazed and decorated with sequins. Just remember that if you are to teach Art and RE in a cross-curricular way, you need to ensure that you simultaneously teach the objectives of Art alongside the objectives of RE.

If you and your KS1 or 2 class choose to make masks out of papier maché, thumb pots for diva lamps out of air-drying clay or Rangoli patterns out of poster paint as part of a festival or celebration, it would be a good idea to explore *why* they are used alongside the *how* they are used within the religion, so that the children learn about the importance of the celebration to the people who follow the faith. To develop AT2, however, it might be worth encouraging the children to consider other art forms that are used to express how a person feels about religious festivals and possibly create their own art that is an expression of how they feel about a secular or religious celebration.

Personal expressions of faith

Mezuzah

People express their personal faith through other forms of practical and useful art. A mezuzah is a Jewish artefact that is a small box and is nailed to the doorpost of a synagogue and every Jewish house. It contains a small manuscript of the Shema, which is a code that the Jewish community live by and is from Deuteronomy 6: 4 onwards. Every time they enter through the doorway, a Jew is expected to touch the mezuzah, and hence the Shema, and remind themselves that God is in everything they do, say and touch. It is a personal expression of their faith. There are many different types of mezuzahs, some of which are very ornate and are decorated with scripture, calligraphy or pattern. The British Library's *Words Alive!* website http://www.blewa.co.uk/project4/teachers/T4-5.htm contains a good thematic art activity with instructions on how to make a basic mezuzah that could be used with a KS1 or 2 class to make a class code of conduct that is similar to the Shema and could be placed on the doorpost of the classroom.

Calligraphy

Islamic art is also a personal expression of faith, as it is believed that it is a visual representation of the divine nature of Allah and the beauty of all He has created (www.bbc.co.uk/religion/religions/islam/art/art_2.shtml). Much Islamic art, such as in architecture, prayer mats and within various Qur'ans, is symmetrical. It is believed by some to be an expression of the infinite nature of Allah and may have no obvious beginning or end. Calligraphy is a style of art that is important in Islam and which can be explored with children, as many of the religious scriptures tend to be hand-written and use calligraphy. Islamic calligraphy is occasionally used to visually express one significant Islamic word or phrase such as one of the *five pillars of Islam* and it helps focus the mind during prayer. Using calligraphy with KS1 or 2 children, explore what their personal life code might be and ask them to create and decorate it. It can then be displayed to remind them and help focus their thoughts during quiet time. There is a wide selection of calligraphy pens available to buy, which are suitable for cross-curricular KS2, although illuminating a manuscript can also be a thematic KS1 activity.

Allegory

Benjamin Hoff explores the allegory of the wine tasters with the philosophy of Taoism. He uses Winnie the Pooh to explain the nuances of Taoism and also explains that a Taoist understands how life may taste bitter or sour at times, but their attitude interprets this differently from other faith traditions (Hoff, 1994:12). It would be useful to use such an allegory with children to discuss what they think about life, whether they agree or disagree with the artist's impression of Buddhism and Confucianism and also to explore if they have a personal philosophy. They could then create their own visual metaphor/allegory that expresses their own ideas about how people view life, e.g. a head teacher, pupil or inspector tasting the broth of school. Although there are some sophisticated concepts here that seem more suitable for KS2, I feel that allegorical pictures can be explained simply so that they can be accessible to KS1 pupils. The example of the thematic art activity is certainly appropriate for both key stages.

National Curriculum and Non Statutory Framework links

RE =	KS1	AT1 1a, 1b, 1d
		AT2 2a, 2b, 2c,
		Breadth of study 3f, 3g, 3h, 3k, 3l, 3o, 3p
	KS2	AT1 1a, 1b, 1d, 1e, 1f
		AT2 2a, 2c, 2e
		Breadth of study 3e, 3i, 3l, 3m, 3n, 3o, 3p, 3r
Art =	KS1	1b, 2a, 2b, 2c, 3a, 4a, 4b, 4c
	KS2	1a, 1b, 2a, 2b, 2c, 3a, 4a, 4b, 4c
	KS1 & 2	Breadth of study 5a, 5b, 5c, 5d

Summary of key points

- There are symbols in art that carry a doctrinal message (iconography)
- Iconography is not limited to Christianity
- Art has been used to put across a religious message for centuries
- Modern art seems to be an expression of an artist's personal faith or their interpretation of a religious concept/event

- Art works well with RE because it naturally causes children to have an opinion
- Art can help children develop language skills so that they are able to communicate emotions about religion and big questions
- There is lots of religious art in buildings, advertising, graphic novels, windows, celebrations, calligraphy and religious texts
- Each artistic style can be explored with children to develop learning about and learning from religion
- Allow children to interpret the art and the religious messages within them so that they create their own expression of religious art using a similar style to the stimulus

Chapter 6
What are the connections between Dance and RE?

LEARNING OBJECTIVES

In this chapter we will consider:

- Creative use of Dance to enhance Religious Education

It will also address elements within the following Standards:

Q3, Q8, Q10, Q14, Q15, Q17, Q18, Q19, Q23, Q25

Introduction

This chapter is written to give you a flavour of how you can creatively connect RE with Dance. It includes a case study of a school I have worked with and a small selection of activity ideas.

RE and Dance

In traditional religions (e.g. African and Melanesian) dance has set formations and rituals that are in pairs, groups or solo and the men seem to play a larger role in the dances than the women. Although I'm generalising here, the men's dances seem to be about war, sun and con-necting to the spirit of animals or ancestors, whereas women's dances seem to be about fertility, harvest, birth rituals, moon worship and mourning (Wosien, 1992; Osterley, 2002). Much folk dance we see in the UK today would have originated from a religion; for example, dancing around the maypole started as a Pagan celebration of Beltane and to celebrate fertility and new life, and Osterley (2002:103) feels that the maypole has a quasi-religious element to it.

Some religions today still see dance and music as worship arts because they set a mood for prayer or meditation. Some Christian denominations have 'Liturgical dance' as a way to help church bodies enhance the worship experience and, according to Thomas Kane as cited in Pardue (2005:65), Liturgical dance seems to have seven aspects, which I have summarised as being mainly about being together and being evangelical. Worship is not designed to be dull and Liturgical dance certainly ensures that laughter is a focus.

There are many ways dance is used in the six major faith traditions around the world, yet it is mainly used as a form of worship or for religious or spiritual uplifting and expression (see Chapter 4). A lovely example of this would be with the monks of Tibet. They dance for a vari-ety of occasions, which at times can include over 100 dancers. They have specially designed costumes and masks that represent man's fight over negative thought and actions and which explore the essence of the Buddhist faith and practices. The monks see the dances as a form of meditation because the monk is in a trance-like state and needs to have a peaceful, focused mind to express the nuances of the dances (Matthieu, 2003). Similarly, the Islamic branch of Sufi dancers in Turkey, commonly known as the Whirling dervishes or Sufi dervishes, spin on the spot and slowly raise their arms to the sky. Their eyes are shut and they too seem to be in a trance. Using a centrifugal force when they spin, the men's skirts lift and look like a plate; it is an amazing spectacle, yet the theology behind the dance is the essence of the dance because they believe that the spinning allows them to spiritually con-nect with God (BBC 2, *Around the World in 80 Faiths*).

Dance seems to be part of religious experience of the past and present and this chapter will explore how you can connect the PE curriculum with Key Skills in RE.

Connecting with the PE curriculum

In the PE section of the National Curriculum there is an area dedicated to Dance under Breadth of study (QCA, 1999:131–3). The skills that the National Curriculum encourages in Dance tend to be about creating personal dances, responding to stimuli, using simple pat-terns and changing pace or rhythm, etc. If you choose to connect PE and RE thematically or in a cross-curricular way, you will need to ensure that the Key Skills of both subjects are addressed.

Below are four examples of how you can translate some religious dances into your PE and RE classroom with practical ideas and case studies. This is, however, not an exhaustive list and much more could be explored within the Dance curriculum.

A themed dance

There are many different types of traditional dance that can be explored with a class, and sometimes it's a good idea to link the dance to a religious theme or geographical region. The *Kathakali* is a story-dance or play originating from Karela in the south-west of India, which has symbolic characters that are *Devas* (gods) or *Asuras* (demons). Dancers use their body to show geometrical patterns, e.g. they stand looking like a square or rectangle with their knees and feet turned outwards or on one foot, and retell a story. The most important parts of the dance, however, are the facial expressions and eye movements. Occasionally the hand and eyes move in a figure of eight and there are jumps, spirals, sweeps and leaps. The *Kathakali* company tour the UK and also provide workshops, so it is worth taking your class to watch them if you can and then invite them into your school (http://www.kathakali.net/).

Jathiswaram is also an Indian cultural dance, but from a different region. It has stylised walks, facial and hand gestures (*mudras*) and fast or slow movements. The dance doesn't tell a story like the *Kathakali*, but is the dancer's expression of the music. There are many clips on YouTube of this dance that can be used with children and which show the distinct nature of the dance.

Activity idea — A Taste of India

The purpose of this dance could be either to retell a religious story from Hinduism, Sikhism or Islam or show/express how they feel about a given piece of music, story or event which could be religious or not. Yet rather than recreate a traditional dance, use it as a stimulus and focus on certain aspects of it such as hand and body positions and the possible meaning behind certain gestures.

Choosing a traditional dance, such as *Jathiswaram* or *Kathakali*, watch a video or DVD clip of it with the children from either KS1 or 2 and then try to break it into distinctive parts whilst in talk partners.

Explore the symbolic nature of *mudras* (Buddhist, Taoist and Hindu symbolic hand gestures) that can be observed in religious art or dance. It would be useful to provide some input on the meanings behind some of the hand gestures so that they realise that messages can be made if you put them together into a phrase. Use art to show how the religion uses the symbolic nature of *mudras*.

Ask the children to explore different hand gestures and upper body movements, using arms, face, legs and torso. Try and encourage them to think of creating a message within the movements that relates to part of the religious story, for example joy, peace and celebration with Holi, or the Diwali story. Experiment with different ways of moving between body parts and hand gestures and then encourage them to explore different speeds and directions.

The next stage would be to connect three movements together into a sequence that contains a message and repeat it three times. Then ask the children to perform to each other so that they can evaluate and refine the movements. Finally, bring in some distinctive music and ask the children to perform their sequence one group after each other so that it becomes a class dance. Rehearse and refine the sequences and then perform them in a class assembly.

National Curriculum and Non Statutory Framework links

RE =	KS1	AT1 1a, 1d
		AT2 2b
		Breadth of study 3f, 3o, 3p
	KS2	AT1 1e, 1g, 1h
		AT2 2b
		Breadth of study 3a, 3g, 3p, 3q, 3r
PE =	KS1	Breadth of study 6a, 6b, 6c, 6d
	KS2	Breadth of study 6a, 6b

Dancing in groups

Group dances that are gender-specific and at times gender-mixed are part of the history of religious dance (Osterley, 2002) and an interesting dynamic to explore with children. The following dance explores some of the traditional ideas of religious dance so that the children interpret the Diwali story in their own way and show this visually through movement. This case study was completed over four lessons that were cross-curricular RE and PE.

Case Study **Communicating knowledge**

Creating a class dance – retelling a story
After undertaking a retelling of the Hindu Diwali story through the use of a Diwali story-telling doll the children divided the story into distinct parts including how Hindus celebrate Diwali today. The parts were as follows:

Part 1 – Rama leaves Sita in magic circle and goes to hunt.

Part 2 – Sita leaves the circle as she hears an animal in distress. She is suddenly kidnapped.

Part 3 – Rama returns and he with his brother Lakshman go looking for her.

Part 4 – Rama asks his friend the Monkey King Hanuman to help because he has a large army.

Part 5 – They all go to save Sita but Ravana's army is ready for them and so a battle began that lasted ten days.

Part 6 – Rama and Sita are reunited and make their way home.

Part 7 – Diwali today. Hindus celebrate with fireworks, singing, dancing, making Rangoli patterns and lighting their houses with lamps.

Using some distinct Indian music that had a regular beat that was downloaded from iTunes (*Dhoom Machale* by Sunidhi Chauhan), the children learnt movements for different parts of the class dance. The intention was to have a set dance with a class beginning, group middle and class end.

The beginning of the dance
After a warm up, the children were divided so that the boys faced the girls. The boys pretended to be warriors like Rama and practised three movements whilst facing the girls

and then froze. The girls pretended to be Sita and practised three movements to the boys and then froze. Then with the music all children did the three movements together. The last part of the music introduction was to move any way they wanted to and travel to different parts of the hall and stay frozen in a freeze frame with a focus group. This was rehearsed a few times so that they became familiar with the music and the distinct drum beat that signalled for a change in movement and position.

The middle of the dance

In their focus groups they created a dance that repeated three movements so that it became a sequence and retold their part of the Hindu story.

They needed to consider four things:

1. Create movements that you can repeat.
2. Use hands, arms and body to create movements.
3. Use different levels, e.g. high or low.
4. Everyone must be involved.

All groups did brilliantly! The focus group that had the most challenging part was group 5 because it was a large group and the children tended to mimic fighting and not interpret war through movement. It was solved by discussing and sharing ideas for the different movements they could do to show fighting, i.e. to show chaos in war by doing the movements at different times to each other. They showed their dances in order to each other and gave suggestions on how to improve the quality of the movements so that the message in the Diwali story was clear.

The end of the dance

The last section was part 7 of the story. It was decided by the class that the ending should include everyone and so the children experimented with showing a festival atmosphere using high and low movements. They could show a celebration in any way possible, but when we came to a certain part of the music they needed to move to the centre of the hall and be a firework at the back (tall children) or a Diva lamp at the front.

The children were enthused to rehearse these sections and the more they became familiar with the music the more their movements improved.

Putting it together

The final session was to put the dance together and work through the transitions from one part to the next. The beginning was refined, then one by one they practised in the focus groups and ended with the celebration dance.

It took a few times to get the dance working sequentially and it wasn't always in time with the music, but it was fun and by the end of the four sessions the children had a good grasp of the Diwali story, had some awareness of how Hindus celebrate Diwali and also had opportunity to reflect on how they feel when they celebrate as a group.

Unfortunately, the class was not able to show this dance to an audience such as an assembly, yet I would suggest that if you ever do create a class dance, one great motivation is purpose. If the children know it is to be performed to an audience then they tend to become more motivated to evaluate, refine and improve the dance, which is a Key Skill in PE (NC 3a, 3b) and also encourages communication and reflection.

Source: Year 1 in a county primary school, Lancashire

National Curriculum and Non Statutory Framework links

RE = KS1	AT1 1a, 1b, 1d
	AT2 2d
	Breadth of Study 3c, 3f, 3g, 3o
PE = KS2	Breadth of study 3a, 3b, 5a, 6a, 6b

Movement with meaning

Religious expression through dance can be easily translated in a practical way into the primary classroom. Liturgical dance tends to be the interpretation and expression of emotions related to religion, yet in the primary classroom you could explore emotions in general, rather than focus directly on feelings about religion.

REToday has lots of good ideas on how to teach RE and their spring 2008 issue explores creativity and how to develop Key Skills through Dance and RE. Liz Tynder (Tynder, 2008) suggests retracing the Hindu shape of *Aum* as part of a class dance and also creating a dance that represents a pilgrimage where the children are the places that a pilgrim would travel through. She also suggests some good top tips on how to teach Dance effectively. Here are four thematic ideas suitable for KS1 and 2 on how to extend a dance through group work and interpretation of lyrics and music.

Interpreting people's faith through movement

Listening to and appraising religious songs such as hymns and mantras can help children begin to see that they are a form of religious expression. Watch a video or DVD clip where they are sung by a variety of people, e.g. by Monks, a gospel choir, a church choir, a congregation, etc. (again YouTube will be a great source for this but you could watch the DVD of *Sister Act* which is now a West End musical or *Songs of Praise* which is on BBC 1 every Sunday evening).

Discuss with the children how people's emotions are evident in the way they are singing and that the hymn or mantra that is being sung is a musical expression of how the people feel. Then ask them to consider what it would look like if we were to translate the song through the body and show how people feel about it.

Ask the children to show through moving their body how they think some of the people on the filmed footage felt about the hymn and discuss why they interpreted the emotion in this way. Show them people who have different expressions when singing as some will look happy, some pious, some bored and some spiritual depending on what film clip you show. This idea can be used as a warm up or be extended into a larger dance whereby a few of the shapes are connected together whilst the hymn is sung.

Interpreting a hymn through movement

In groups give the children a selection of hymns that they are familiar with (http://www.hymnlyrics.org/). Christmas carols are usually a good starting point in a community school because the children may not be familiar with religious songs but are likely to know carols. Ask them to work out what they believe to be the message in the hymn, then using three movements that they repeat in a sequence, ask them to interpret the hymn through movement extending so that they have a starting and end position either side of their sequence. Once they have had enough time to discuss, explore, evaluate and refine their interpretations ask them to perform them using the music to the rest of the group. Remember to match the language of the hymn to the children's age group and capabilities.

Words in hymns

This idea can be extended further into a class or another group dance by looking at particular words within religious songs and exploring what they mean, e.g. joyful, alleluia, triumphant, amazing, hark, praise, etc; the children should first explore what the words mean by using a mind map and then explore different body positions that relate to them. In pairs ask them to put their three body movements together with the music and create a sequence of six positions. Finally as a class, talk about how all the positions seen can be used to interpret a whole hymn and explore the purpose of a hymn.

A class dance with words and movement

Play a hymn and show the lyrics to the children then plan together which three to six movements they think would be good to put into a sequence to represent the message of the hymn (focus on the chorus to start). Practise them together as a class, then agree when they all should change body position so that they don't change at different times. Play the hymn and direct the children to change and move positions at certain times. This could then be extended into different groups who take a verse each and create their own sequence. Finally, put all sequences and verses together as a class dance.

National Curriculum and Non Statutory Framework links

RE = KS1	AT1 1d, 1e	
	AT2 2a	
	Breadth of study 3a, 3g, 3o, 3q	
KS2	AT1 1e, 1g, 1h	
	AT2 2b	
	Breadth of study 3a, 3g, 3p, 3q, 3r	
PE = KS1	Breadth of study 3a, 3b, 3c, 6a, 6b, 6c, 6d	
KS2	Breadth of study 3a, 3b, 5a, 6a, 6b	

Sacred dance

The best way to understand liturgical, cultural or religious dance is through observing it, so it's a good idea if you can arrange for a touring dance company to visit your school or take your children out to visit a religious community where dance happens as a form of worship. This is ideal when some dances are considered sacred and part of the practice of worship.

The monk dancers of Tibet have many sacred dances, and Tai Chi is also considered by some to be a form of meditative dance. Each movement is conducted and put together to become a symbolic representation of the philosophy Taoism or way of life.

There are other cultural and ritual dances within various communities such as the Irish Ceilidh and festival dances for Purim in Judaism. There are also ceremonial dances, e.g. the *Hora* dance which is performed during a Jewish wedding. In this dance, the guests hold a handkerchief between each other so that it forms a chain and then lift the bride and groom on chairs as a symbolic representation that they are king and queen for the day. The *Krenzl* dance, however, is where the mother of the bride is crowned with flowers and her daughters dance around her as a celebration of all daughters being married.

Furthermore, some Christian schools in the UK are currently exploring the concepts of religion and worship through dance with primary children. David Briggs, a head teacher in Warwickshire, explores in *REtoday* (2009:36) how his school uses dance with children as a method of developing and understanding religious worship so as to become unified in the expression of their faith. He also found that the liturgical dance that was experienced in his school not only helped children's spiritual development but also had a positive effect on learning within other subjects.

Each dance, whether it is cultural, ritual or sacred, is an expression of how the people feel about either their faith or about the event that is taking place. This can be explored with KS1 and 2 children by creating their own set dance piece for a celebratory event or by learning a traditional dance and recreating it. They could also create their own movement dance that is inspired by scripture and dance it regularly on special occasions such as at the start or end of term or on a birthday. Yet it is important to be aware that to teach cross-curricular Dance and RE you must remember to develop the skills of both subjects simultaneously in the lesson.

Summary of key points

- Dance is a form of worship and is called liturgical dance
- Dance is an expression of man's relationship with God and has been linked to religion for centuries. We can find evidence of this in religious art
- Men and women have different roles in religious and cultural dance
- There are many different types of religious dance such as dances for festival and celebrations (the Jewish festival of Purim and within Jewish wedding celebrations)
- Around the world we can see dances that encourage a spiritual connection with God (Islamic Sufi dervishes and monk dancers of Tibet)
- There are a variety of ways of using dance to develop the RE skills of reflection, communication and interpretation. They can be:
  - Through a themed dance - recreate or take elements from a traditional dance and produce your own
  - Retelling a religious story through a class dance
  - Dancing in pairs then groups so as to connect three movements that translate (using body movements) the meaning behind words and messages in hymns
  - Some schools in the UK are exploring Dance as a way to enhance religious understanding. Look at *REtoday* for further ideas

Chapter 7

What are the connections between Drama and RE?

LEARNING OBJECTIVES

In this chapter we will consider:

- Creative use of Drama to enhance Religious Education

It will also address elements within the following Standards:

Q3, Q8, Q10, Q14, Q15, Q17, Q18, Q19, Q23, Q25

Introduction

This chapter explores how Religious Education can be taught creatively with Drama. It includes some real case studies of schools and teachers I have worked with and a small selection of activity ideas.

RE and Drama

Unlike Art, Dance and Music, Drama isn't obvious in ancient artwork or scripture, yet it is a tool that some religious denominations use as a means to explore religious understanding and worship. Goens (1999) provides a comprehensive guide on how to use drama within worship and offers suggestions on ways to explore scripture through part reading, choral reading, storytelling, etc. (1999:33–67). She implies that the arts are for all of the community and should not be reserved for children during festivals because some of the concepts within a religion need opportunity for personal reflection and exploration. Therefore, arts such as sacred dance and drama can support an individual's spiritual journey, no matter what age they may be.

In the UK we tend to see Drama and RE explicitly linked at Christmas where many schools justify the suspension of other subjects so that they can rehearse for the end of term play or assembly for parents. In my experience, this time can be stressful for teachers and children, and yet it seems that the Key Stage 1 Nativity play is a form of religious entertainment that will not go away. Today, we can buy ready-made costumes such as the star and shepherds in well known supermarkets thereby proving that it is a given in the British society that at Christmas, adults will enjoy seeing their children retell the Christian Christmas story and also explore some secular concepts of giving and receiving.

However, against the advice of Goens (ibid.) the Nativity play in schools today does not seem to explore religious concepts, Personal Learning and Thinking Skills or personal ideologies and belief systems and possibly is not used to its best advantage. Once a year at least, schools in the UK have a captive audience in the parents and children and this could be the one opportunity to teach good Religious Education and make it stand apart from the other subjects. However, teachers seem not to use it to develop the skills and understandings of Religious Education and investigate the what, why, where, when, who and how of Christmas or even explore it in conjunction with other Light Festivals, which is a little disappointing.

Christmas plays and Nativity plays can encourage creativity and enjoyment, but teachers should not simply use this time to learn and rehearse a play that they have purchased, but should use it to develop thinking skills, create their own class play and, yet more importantly, encourage personal reflection on the themes and messages within the Christian Christmas story.

I feel that Drama should not be kept for Christmas, but should be used within most RE lessons. It should be used to create and improve Key Skills in RE: as a way to develop empathy, understanding, answer puzzling questions and achieve Attainment Targets 1 and 2. This can be explored at Christmas, but also at any time of the year.

Connecting with the English curriculum

English within the National Curriculum has an area focused on Drama within Speaking and Listening in both Key Stages 1 and 2. It expects children to participate in a wide range of drama activities, explore stories, characters, emotions and work with others. The *Non Statutory Framework for RE* also expects children to use dramatic conventions such as stories to explore aspects of religion, hence both subjects seem to have similar links to Key Skills (McCreery *et al.*, 2008:38–53).

Below are four examples of how you can translate some dramatic techniques into your RE and English classroom with practical ideas and case studies.

Dramatic conventions

There are a variety of dramatic techniques that can encourage empathy and consideration of how people feel about an event or concept or even help children explore how they feel.

Persona dolls

The persona doll is similar to a rag doll, but does not have a face or clothing, so it can be used in a variety of ways with KS1 and 2. One such way could be to explore religious and cultural identity, e.g., what would a person wear to show they belong, which could then be related to the 5Ks of Sikhism (see Chapter 12). Children could also use it to re-enact religious stories such as the Hindu Diwali story, explore religious settings such as the flight to Egypt or Jesus in the wilderness or religious events and celebrations such as baptism. You could also use the dolls to explore how the children feel about big questions such as death or anger, and the doll could be used to answer for the child. The persona doll is ideal for use in Key Stage 1 and Early Years (Bowles, 2004), for example, in a role-play area or within an imaginative play setting, but is also suitable for older children and story-telling.

* clothing

The Godly play

The Godly play is a prescribed method of retelling a story from the Christian Bible. Using symbols, objects and open-ended questions, the storyteller encourages the children to reflect on what they think about an event within the story and relate it to personal experience. Its purpose is to help children consider their own ideas about religion and religious messages in stories and to think about what they believe about faith. The technique of the Godly play is an interesting approach to use in exploring stories from Christianity, but I believe it can also be used with other faith traditions because it explicitly encourages Personal Learning and Thinking Skills through reflection rather than question and answer sessions. See www.godlyplay.org.uk for more details.

Hot seating

This technique is great for exploring opinions, emotions and developing empathy with characters. The case study below demonstrates how this technique can be used with children of all ages and capabilities and can also help explore some challenging concepts.

> ## Case Study   Communicating knowledge
>
> ### Hot seating the Hitler Youth
> Whilst working as a Museum Education Officer at The British Library, I designed and delivered a workshop about children during World War II that used the collections in the gallery. One of the activities was to create a letter as a child who was part of the Hitler Youth during 1939. As a method to help the children understand what to write in the letter, the children first explored how it would feel to be segregated from their family and live in a summer camp, have their letters home screened and be directed to behave and think in a certain way.
>
> Each child was given a prepared question and sat in a semi-circle, whilst one child volunteered to sit on a chair at the front and respond to the questions. Having each child with a

specific question allowed them all to participate and develop enough confidence to ask another if they wished.

The outcome was amazing. An autistic boy (B), who was 12 and working at Level 2 in writing, volunteered to be in the hot seat and when he sat down and started acting his role, his whole demeanour changed. He became a certain type of character and demonstrated a very good understanding of the Hitler Youth project and some of the feelings some children may have felt about being away from home. His responses inspired more in-depth questions that explored the emotions of other people about some of the events of the war.

This developed into a class discussion about what happened to children during wartime, whether evacuation was necessary, why anti-Semitism is wrong and allowed them to develop their own points of view. The teacher explained that the hot seating approach helped B consider other viewpoints, which was a difficulty of his, and she was impressed with how much he and the others had learnt from each other.

Source: Year 8 Moderate Learning Difficulty School, North London (working at level 2, 3 and 4 for English yet had a variety of emotional, learning, physical and behavioural issues)

Exploring dilemmas

One of the difficult, but also interesting, aspects of RE is that there is always more than one answer to big questions. Personal responses to any question will have been affected by culture, upbringing and religion. It is, therefore, a good idea to try and explore such issues through a dramatic technique so that children can reflect on what they know and understand and decide for themselves. Below are some good techniques to help children understand characters within religious stories.

Conscience alley

This helps explore a character's emotions and decision making process. For example, the class stand opposite each other and are in character as the crowd at Jesus' trial. Another child, who is in character as Pilate, walks through a gap that they have made. Whilst they walk through the gap, one side of the class give reasons for crucifying Jesus, while the other side tries to persuade Pilate not to. All children have to stay in character. By the time Pilate reaches to the end of the alley, the class will have heard and explored all arguments and be aware of the dilemma that he faced. This can be created with any character within a religious story or even themselves if they want to work out how they feel about a given issue (such as whether to steal) and is suitable for KS1 or 2.

Corner running

This can be used for a similar purpose to the technique above, where children need to make a decision. Options are placed in the four corners of the room and children run or walk to the option they think is the most important. Eventually, you can narrow it down so that you come to a collective decision. A good KS1 example of this is on www.teachers.tv (*Big Ideas for Small People*).

Expert groups and snowballing

Expert groups is a device that can be useful for AT1, because the children are divided into groups of four and are given a topic to become an expert in, such as one group learns about *Salat* and another about *Hajj* (which are two of the five pillars of Islam). The children are then re-grouped so that there is one expert on each topic in the new group. One expert teaches the others in their new group about their specialism and the others do the same in turn. They then have to produce a group outcome such as a report, essay, presentation, poster, etc. that uses all the information gathered. This technique develops knowledge of the subject matter and ensures that all children are involved.

Snowballing is similar to expert grouping, yet this is usually where a pair discusses a topic and then joins another pair so that they make a new group of four and discuss the same topic. This four then joins another four to make eight and discuss the topic and then eight with another eight, and so on. Each time the children discuss and refine their ideas to come to a collective opinion, if possible. The objective of such a technique is to listen to answers and opinions and put across their own. It encourages KS1 and 2 children to come to informed opinions.

National Curriculum and Non Statutory Framework links

RE =	KS1	AT1 1a, 1c, 1d,
		AT2 1a, 1b,
		Breadth of study 3i, 3n, 3o, 3p
	KS2	AT1 1a, 1e, 1f, 1g, 1h
		AT2 2a, 2b, 2c, 2d
		Breadth of study 3h, 3j, 3m, 3o, 3r
English = Drama =	KS1	4a, 4b
	KS2	4a, 4b, 4c
	KS1 & 2	Breadth of study speaking, drama activities

Group drama

There are a variety of ways to develop group work in drama. The following examples are great methods to explore characters in religious stories, retell stories, retell specific religious events and explore emotions to develop knowledge. They are suitable for KS1 and 2.

Freeze frame

This is an activity where the children are in groups of about six and are given an event such as the Jewish Passover story or the ten plagues of Moses. They have to create a visual representation of the event and then freeze it. Each child is a specific character and stands in a certain way with the others in the group so as to tell the story visually. The teacher then unfreezes one child at a time to explore what is happening and how their character feels about the event.

Powered body sculpture

This is similar to freeze frame, but retells a story through a child moving the arms, legs, facial expressions and body positions of a different child or three children in their visual sculpture

(Mackley and Draycott, 2000:12). They retell a religious story such as Hanukkah to the rest of the class through different positions of their sculpture. It is easier to do this in groups of no more than three.

Role play and shadow puppets

This technique encourages the children to retell a religious story through becoming the characters or making the characters and re-enacting the events in the story. *The First Christmas* by Pienkowski (2006) is an excellent children's book that recounts the Christmas story and uses beautiful shadow puppet illustrations. It would be a great starting point for this technique.

Television shows

Using hand-held cameras or digital blue cameras, the children could write a script and film themselves presenting it or create an animation. They could do it from a variety of approaches, such as a simple retelling of a religious story, interviewing certain characters within it and then creating a news programme or a modern twist on the story and produce a news piece that is related to issues today. Using a *City Learning Centre* might be an idea so that the children can learn how to use the editing facilities and create a joint partnership project.

National Curriculum and Non Statutory Framework links

RE =	KS1	AT1 1a, 1c, 1d
		AT2 1a, 1e
		Breadth of study 3f, 3h, 3n, 3o, 3q
	KS2	AT1 1a, 1b, 1e, 1f, 1g
		AT2 2a, 2c, 2d
		Breadth of study 3e, 3m, 3o, 3p, 3r
English = Drama =	KS1	4a, 4b, 4c
	KS2	4a, 4b, 4c, 4d
	KS1 & 2	Breadth of study speaking, drama activities

Class drama

Class drama is similar to group drama and many of the conventions and techniques explored above can be used within class dramas. The difference, however, is that it can help children develop their skills in performance and improvisation, thus making it a cross-curricular lesson.

Choral reading

Choral reading is where children read a poem or piece of prose in unison. There are many ways of doing this, but the main thing to consider is how to structure the various parts. Consider how you want the children to stress certain words and phrases and choose groups to read particular parts in turn and other parts to read as a class.

To develop this idea into a religious context, explore with the children why people who follow a faith speak in unison when they are reinforcing their fundamental beliefs such as during the 'Nicene Creed' and 'the Lord's Prayer' in Christianity; Hindu and Sikh mantras and Buddhist chants.

Courtroom drama

One way of developing improvisation would be to create a courtroom drama where the children decide to put a biblical character on trial such as Abraham for the attempted murder of his son Isaac, Noah for stealing animals, Judas for betrayal or even Jesus himself. The children have to provide prosecution and defence and a group will have to be the jury. Obviously this concept is more suitable for top Key Stage 2, but it can be simplified for Key Stage 1, depending on the chosen character and the capabilities of your class.

Class improvisation

As has been mentioned early in this chapter, children are expected to put on a class performance at Christmas time and also during class assemblies. The Nativity story can be explored in many different ways to develop understanding of the events, characters and religious meaning. Below is a case study of how Alison Jarvis (an RE Coordinator) used a class improvisation to develop understanding with a KS1 class about how Jesus' birth affected people at the time.

Case Study

Alison wanted the children to sequence the Christmas story and consider the emotions of the characters. She encouraged the children to retell the different parts of the story from the perspective of the different characters. She started by dividing the children into groups and providing them with the costumes from the box that is reserved for the traditional Nativity play production within the school. Once the children put on the costumes she encouraged them to consider how those characters felt about hearing the news of Jesus' birth.

She then asked them to create a freeze frame about the characters and present it so that it showed the character's emotion. Once they had had an opportunity to rehearse their frame the children were asked to present it and she then unfroze some of the characters so that they could explain what they were thinking and feeling. The children also used the school's digital blue cameras to take pictures of the frames.

The final part of the lesson was then to sequence the events of the story using the digital blue images. Returning to the traditional story, the children worked out the order of the freeze frame images and thus the sequence of the events within the Christmas story. Using the images as a stimulus they discussed the similar emotions between the characters and why possibly they might have felt this way, they then recorded such emotions using laminated speech and thought bubbles and placed them with the images. This activity was extended into other lessons so that the children could retell the Christmas story from a different perspective.

Alison Jarvis Year 2 class teacher and RE coordinator, St Thomas Chequerbent CV Primary School, Bolton

Although some religious traditions do use drama for worship (Goens, 1999; Osterley, 2002), it is mainly used for religious expression or story-telling. I recommend, however, that when retelling, recounting or re-enacting a religious story, you should allow the children to do it from their own understanding of it and allow them to choose the content. The festival of

Purim is an excellent example of how the Jewish community explore their faith through drama and interpret it on a personal basis. It is based on the book of Esther and, for the reading in the synagogue, some congregations dress up and take an active part through re-enacting the story and make noises when certain characters are read aloud. It looks similar to a pantomime, but there is a theological perspective that underpins the activities.

When using stories with children, I recommend that you retell rather than read a text with children as this way you will become a good role model for how to retell and recount (a Key Skill in English), but you will also make the story more real and interesting to the children as you are likely to embellish parts of it and stress others. Retelling is the natural art form for drama.

National Curriculum and Non Statutory Framework links

RE =	KS1	AT1 1a, 1c, 1d
		AT2 1a, 1e
		Breadth of study 3f, 3h, 3n, 3o, 3q
	KS2	AT1 1a, 1b, 1e, 1f, 1g
		AT2 2a, 2c, 2d
		Breadth of study 3e, 3m, 3o, 3p, 3r
English =	KS1	4a, 4b, 4c
	KS2	4a, 4b, 4c, 4d
	KS1 & 2	Breadth of study speaking, drama activities

Summary of key points

- Religion uses drama for worship and retelling religious stories
- Drama is a good method to use when you wish to explore emotions
- There are a variety of dramatic conventions that are useful for RE
  - Persona dolls
  - The Godly play
  - Hot seating
  - Exploration of dilemmas
  - Conscience alley
  - Corner running
  - Freeze frame
  - Powered sculpture
  - Role play
  - TV shows
  - Improvisation
- Consider how to group children when exploring Drama and RE especially when using choral reading
- Retell rather than read stories

Chapter 8
What are the connections between Music and RE?

LEARNING OBJECTIVES

In this chapter we will consider:

- Creative use of Music to enhance Religious Education

It will also address elements within the following Standards:

Q3, Q8, Q10, Q14, Q15, Q17, Q18, Q19, Q23, Q25

Introduction

This chapter is written to give you a flavour of how you can creatively connect RE with Music. It includes some real case studies of schools and teachers I have worked with and a small selection of activity ideas.

RE and Music

As discussed in the previous chapters, most religions have had a close relationship with music throughout history, and it is frequently used as a way for people to worship, express their faith and/or interpret how they feel. Many different instruments are used, although there seem to be a few that are common to many religions, namely drums, rattles/shakers of some kind and stringed instruments, such as guitars and sitars. Such instruments can be easily found in schools, but it is important to note that religious music is not restricted to this. The musical scores for Mozart's *Requiem Mass* and Handel's *Messiah* require a full orchestra, but also include specifications for vocal instruments, i.e. a choir and so it is important to allow your class to use their voice as an instrument too.

Connecting with the Music curriculum

In the Music section of the National Curriculum (NC) children are expected to perform, compose, appraise and listen (QCA, 1999:124-7). Each of these skills can be applied to the Key Skills of Religious Education and utilised to help explore Attainment Target 2 (Learning From Religion) of the *Non Statutory Framework for RE* (QCA, 2004). Below are a few examples with case studies on how to develop Personal Learning and Thinking Skills through cross-curricular and thematic RE and Music.

Creating and performing music

If you are not a music specialist, it can seem daunting to use instruments with children and create or perform music, yet there are many resources available to support you. The Music Manifesto website (http://www.musicmanifesto.co.uk/) provides lots of information on courses, general focus groups and a general direction for schools to take in relation to music learning and teaching. Also *Sing Up* is a national singing programme linked to the manifesto that has a fantastic bank of resources, ideas and courses for all teachers (http://www.singup.org/), which can help you develop your knowledge and understanding of the value of music teaching with Personal Learning and Thinking Skills. Using both websites, you will be able to improve your confidence enough to possibly try using the noisy things whose names you don't know and which are stacked in the corner of the room!

However, combining Music with RE can be a useful way to build confidence as it can seem less worrying if you are meeting the objectives of two subjects through a familiar approach that has a focus on not being a great musician but simply a musical person. As the previous chair for National Association of Music Educators (NAME) believes 'everyone has the capacity to express themselves through music' (Harrison, 2008:1). Therefore, this is what we focus on with RE and Music: expressing personal emotion, understanding and reflection.

There are many cross-curricular and thematic ways of producing good quality musical learning without having to be able to be grade 8 on the piano. The examples provided below expect you to have some basic understanding of the music curriculum and range from easy to fairly tricky. However, lack of knowledge should never stop you from having a go at being creative.

Simple to manage – body sounds

Music is basically a collection of sounds that can be interpreted in a variety of ways. A simple way to start is to explore body sounds. Sounds that are loud and soft, such as clapping, ticking, clicking, clucking, scratching, shh-ing, etc., which the children can control.

Start with four different sounds and divide the class into four groups. Each group is responsible for a certain body sound. Using hand signals, direct the groups to start making their sound and signal when to stop. Develop this so that there is an order to which group starts, who is next and when to stop altogether. Finally, increase the difficulty so they practise with quiet sounds building to a crescendo and ending towards silence. In essence, your role will be to orchestrate when the groups start, how loud they should be and when they all end.

This can be linked to RE through using a creation story such as exploring the sound of Aum and the sounds of creation; exploring a religious festival and how it is celebrated or producing the atmosphere for an event that is written in a sacred text.

Not so difficult to manage – make your own song

Making your own song isn't as difficult as it sounds. The best way to start is to choose a familiar tune such as 'Jingle Bells' or 'Silent Night' and look at the meter, rhyme and syllables in each line of the chorus. Using a theme, for example *We are special, Forgiveness* or *God Loves Us*, change the words of the chorus but keep the melody. Create a class chorus and then group verses. Below is a case study of a trainee teacher at Edge Hill University who experimented with the idea of RE and Music which explores how she created a class song using the melody of 'Jingle Bells'.

Case Study — Communicating knowledge

Below is a case study describing how a trainee teacher at Edge Hill University experimented with the idea of RE and Music to create a class song using the melody of 'Jingle Bells'. They sang it as a class and then talked through the various parts of the structure. She explored how, when a song is sung the chorus is repeated a few times, and reinforced that it is the part of the song that puts across the main message whereas the verses generally further develop a story, feeling or message.

Taking this idea further she asked the children to work in talk partners and, using white boards, come up with a possible couplet for the first part of the chorus based on a theme which was the objective taken from the Lancashire Scheme of work. After some time and some support with understanding the syllables within the lines, she collected some ideas from the children and chose one example which became the first part of the class chorus. She asked them to repeat this for the next part of the chorus and then listened to their ideas. Again she chose a good rhyming couplet and put it together into the chorus. The class then sang the new words using the old melody.

Within the second part of the lesson, Katie snowballed the mixed ability pairs into groups of four and extended the activity. Each group had large pieces of paper and were encouraged to create a verse using the old melody. Each group had a slightly different focus for their verse. Katie used the other adults in the classroom and herself to support children who were having trouble finding rhyme or syllables to match the melody. Frequently, she reminded the children of the melody so that they could make sure they understood what they were doing and could sing it.

In the plenary the groups sang their verse as a way to perform and present the message in their song and the whole class punctuated them with the class chorus.

Source: Katie Warwick trainee teacher on Developmental Placement Year 3/4 children in a primary school, Lancashire

Fairly tricky to manage – composing music

This would be more than one lesson. Notation and composing is a difficult concept and if, like me, you are unable to read music, it can seem daunting to try and develop this concept with children. The simplest way of doing this is to take a theme such as love, hope, joy and ask the children to choose the best selection of instruments to recreate what the word or theme means to them. So, for example, they could use a triangle and bells to sound joyful or a cymbal that they could crash loudly. Encourage the children to qualify why they suggested their instrument.

The next stage is to put the children into mixed ability groups of about four and give them a word or theme to focus on. They need first to choose an instrument (one each) then discuss a way of reproducing a short piece of music with a clear beginning, middle and end. They need to consider whether the instruments are played simultaneously within certain points of the piece. Obviously, you will need to discuss tempo, composition and how to organise who plays when and what, etc.

The children then need to write down their ideas, and a simple way would be to use a symbol for each instrument; this is a simple form of notation called graphic notation or graphic scores. They then note the order in which they are going to play so that it becomes a visual representation of which instrument is being played, for how long and when. It will be clear which instruments are being played simultaneously from the visual score.

The children then test out their composition to see if it sounds right and if not, they change their notations. They then practise to refine and eventually perform to each other.

Introducing a religious story as a stimulus (for example Jesus in the Wilderness or the story of Buddha's enlightenment) and exploring the emotions and events through music can develop into a religious piece of music. The children will be able to perform music using the graphic score to show emotions and events within the story.

National Curriculum and Non Statutory Framework links

RE =	KS1	AT1 1a, 1d, 1e, 1g
		AT2 2a, 2c
		Breadth of study 3h, 3n, 3o, 3p, 3q
	KS2	AT1 1b, 1e, 1h
		AT2 2a, 2c, 2e
		Breadth of study 3l, 3o, 3p, 3q, 3r, 3s
Music =	KS1	1a, 1b, 1c, 2a, 2b, 3a, 3b, 4b, 4c, 4d
		Breadth of study 5a, 5c, 5d
	KS2	1a, 1b, 1c, 2a, 2b, 3a, 3b, 3c, 4b, 4c, 4d
		Breadth of study 5a, 5b, 5c, 5e

Interpreting and appraising music

There are many religious songs available for children to explore and consider the meaning behind them. Contemporary Christian singer-song writer Amy Grant (www.amygrant.com) provides a wealth of music that shows her interpretation of what it means to be a Christian. Similarly Islamic singer-song writer Sami Yusuf (www.samiyusuf.com) also produces songs that are mainly about his faith and is becoming very popular amongst the Islamic community. Such music can help children begin to see how people use music as a form of religious expression.

Asking children to interpret the lyrics of a religious or non-religious song and consider what they think of it, including how the song makes them feel, can help children improve the Key Skills of communication and reflection.

How to encourage a child to interpret and appraise music will be explored here through a variety of cross-curricular and thematic lesson ideas and a case study.

Desert Island Discs

This is a fantastic programme that began on BBC Radio 4 in 1942. Celebrities such as Prime Ministers of the time, actors, writers, etc. are asked to imagine they are castaways on an island and choose eight pieces of music that they would take with them. The music needs to be relevant to them and also say something about their life story or how they feel about current affairs. The programme is edited then broadcast on Radio 4 and finally placed on the BBC website http://www.bbc.co.uk/radio4/factual/desertislanddiscs.shtml. The *Desert Island Disc* programme offers an insight into the personal life of that person and their fundamental beliefs.

This could be a wonderful opportunity for KS1 and 2 children to relate music to meaning. If they were each asked to choose four songs (religious or not) to present to the class and were required to interpret what each song meant to them, they would need to use the skills of communication, interpretation, reflection, personal expression, thinking and applying. The presentation could be created in a variety of ways such as a general presentation for circle time. But better yet, it would be a great idea to use the technology available and create a real radio recording or podcast. Using digital recorders the children could interview each other and then the recordings, once edited, could be put onto a CD for the class reading corner or library or uploaded onto the school website with a specially designed web page.

The children who listen to and present the recordings would develop the skills of open-mindedness, respect, reflection and possibly enquiry, as the songs chosen may raise questions that require further debate and class discussion, which are all higher order thinking skills and thus make this lesson more interesting. Kinnaird (2008:33) and Langan (2008:23) explore this concept a little further and have experimented in their own classrooms with creative approaches to teaching RE using digital technology and *REtoday* offers classroom materials in their Autumn issue (Blaycock, 2008).

Interpretation of music

Other ways of interpreting songs or hymns would be to look closely at lyrics. Some songs such as *What if God was One of Us?*, by Joan Osbourne, and *Jesus Loves Me*, by Anna B. Warner, have been sung by many different artists and interpreted in different ways yet the lyrics have not altered. The Internet is a good place to start to find original and subsequent versions of religious songs that can be downloaded in an MP3 format.

Using a variety of interpretations with the children and then discussing which version they prefer, and why, will help children begin to see that musical scores are a way of interpreting lyrics, and also that religious songs (or songs with religious connotations) are ways of expressing and exploring a person's faith. In some cases, the lyrics may be a form of religious expression, but the score and the interpretation of it may develop this expression to become spiritually uplifting or solemn. Through listening to a variety of songs and versions and through having the opportunity to discuss meaning, children will begin to practise the skill of appraisal.

The following case study shows how a song that has many versions was used as a way to develop interpretation of music and reflection on who God is.

Case Study

Interpreting lyrics – What if God Was One of Us? (By Joan Osbourne). Version sung by the Artist formerly known as Prince from the album *Emancipation* (NPG Records)

The children had explored various versions of the song prior to this session. They looked at the song throughout the years starting with the original from the 1960s. In this lesson they were exploring one final modern version and interpreting what may have influenced the artist to present the lyrics in the way they chose.

The children reviewed the lyrics of 'What if God was One of Us?' and listened to the version by the Artist formerly known as Prince. Whilst listening, they made notes on what they thought of it. They discussed in talking partners what they liked and didn't like about the version, then finally considered (out of all the versions heard so far) which version they preferred and why.

During the class discussion, children were asked to consider why they liked particular versions and discussed how the instruments used and the various tempos had an effect on the style of the song and therefore its meaning.

The children then looked at the lyrics again and, using them as evidence, discussed the writer's view of God. They discussed how and why God could be a slob, a hard worker or an ordinary person as the lyrics suggest. Asking the children 'Would God have been alone?' as is written in the lyrics, the children responded by stating;

'No because He's God!'
'Maybe, because He hasn't got his disciples yet.'
'Maybe He hasn't got a mobile phone.'
'Maybe He is poor 'cause God was poor in the Bible and so hasn't got a home to live in and so no friends.'

The children were then asked to draw what they think God would look like if he lived in St Helen's today and list His characteristics. Many of the children drew Him as a homeless person and similar to the traditional Western image of Jesus. None of the children drew Him as a woman or wealthy.

'This is God singing'

The lesson ended with the classroom organised into a circle. Using the question raised within the lyrics, the children were directed to ask God one question and share with the class. Again, the responses were enlightening as they showed that current global issues of the environment, racial difference and war are real concerns to young children today:

'Why is there war?'
'Why did you go away?'
'Are you God of everything or just Christians?'
'Can my dog live forever like me?'
'Can you stop the World from dying?'

Source: Year 2/3 in a Church of England primary school, Merseyside

This lesson could be extended further to explore the person of Jesus and God and in particular link to images of Jesus using Margaret Cooling's fantastic resource; *Jesus Through Art* (1999).

Listening to music

Listening to and interpreting music is a skill that is encouraged in the National Curriculum's Music Programmes of Study (QCA, 1999: 124-6). David Hay suggests that listening to music can be a way of achieving a spiritual experience (Hay, 2008:4-5) and the Scottish composer/conductor, James McMillan, presented a paper for the Sandford St Martin Trust on 1 October 2008, which was then aired on BBC Radio 4, that stated that there is a definite affinity between religion and music and that composers when creating music are spiritually developing themselves and society (2008:3). He developed his paper to say that taking time to actively listen to music could be seen as a form of meditation and prayer because, 'something of the essence of ourselves is sacrificed' (2008:5). Listening to music can be a spiritually uplifting experience and so schools should make time to listen to and be inspired by religious music.

Listening to music does not always have to be scheduled in a timetable. Whenever there is a gap in the day, a piece of music can be played; as background in the library or as an activity in the reading area. It can also become a set lesson where the objective is to respond sensitively to spiritual music. Interpretation of and response to music can be presented in a variety of ways, and in this instance it is even more important not to stifle the child's creativity, but allow them to provide a personal response in their own way.

It is important to remember that creativity is about *being creative* and *learning creatively* (see Chapter 1) and so a child could demonstrate their ideas and opinions of music and RE through:

- Thought bubbles
- Pieces of art, e.g. pastels, sculpture, drawings, sewing
- Talk partners
- Thinking book
- Drama
- Dance
- Song
- Poetry
- Blog or/and podcast (Bushell, 2009)
- Radio review
- Silence

National Curriculum and Non Statutory Framework links

RE =	KS1	AT2 2b, 2e
		Breadth of study 3n, 3o, 3p, 3q
	KS2	AT1 1b, 1e, 1h
		AT2 2c, 2e
		Breadth of study 3l, 3o, 3p, 3q, 3r, 3s
Music =	KS1	3a, 4b, 4c, 4d
		Breadth of study 5a, 5c, 5d
	KS2	4b, 4c, 4d
		Breadth of study 5b, 5c, 5e

Spiritual music

There are various definitions of what spiritual music is. Spiritual music can be music without lyrics; containing instruments such as bells, pipes and a slow tempo whereas some people would claim it is music that has an explicitly religious nature (McMillan, 2008). Either way, music that helps create a calm atmosphere or spirit is usually seen as spiritual. Such music is usually used for some religious ceremonies and during meditation, Tai Chi, yoga and relaxation therapies.

Singing or chanting in a group is wonderfully uplifting. It is amazing how it can create a sense of identity and belonging. The National Curriculum Programmes of Study for Music (NC KS1 and 2 1a, 1c) suggest that children should be taught how to sing in unison and chant in parts (QCA, 1999:124, 126).

There are a variety of ways to develop choral singing or chanting; below are two examples.

Choral reading/singing

Choose a hymn that has a poetic rhythm and a story or a strong message such as *Holy Holy Holy* (Reginald Heber 1783-1826), 'It's Me, it's Me, it's Me, Oh Lord' (anon) or *Peace is Flowing like a River* (anon). You can obtain lyrics to Christian hymns from some good websites such as http://www.hymnlyrics.org; http://www.hymnsite.com and http://www.stmarysbaldock.fsnet.co.uk/hymns/, yet you might want to consider using mantras and poems from other faith traditions.

However, before you share the hymn or religious poem with the children, it is best to consider the following points so that you are organised and know how to develop a sense of unity through choral reading, chanting and singing.

1. How will you divide the text into distinct parts? For example if a line is repeated, one half the class says it first then is it repeated by the other half, or will you divide the class into groups and each group take one verse and then the final verse everyone speaks together?

2. How will you say certain words so that the meaning is stressed? For example will you shout, whisper, slow down etc. on specific words such as holy or Alleluia?

3. Will you use the score? If you intend to eventually sing the hymn then having the musical score is useful and you can build up from choral chanting to choral singing. Yet occasionally if you do not sing the hymn it is lovely to share what it does sound like when a professional choir sings it.

Once you have decided how you intend to organise the choral reading or singing, rehearse it with the children. Read it first with them then explore what certain words mean to them and to a religious person. Regularly practise speaking in time with each other and practise how to stress words and alter the volume at specific times. Eventually build up so that you present in a class assembly to the rest of the school and parents.

Chanting – the sacred sound of Aum

Many eastern religions use chanting as a form or worship, and usually this can help focus the mind during meditation. Playing with various tones can be a lovely activity when exploring the concept of Om or Aum. In one of the creation stories in the Hindu tradition, the world was created by a sound (believed to be the sound of Aum) resonating throughout the universe. Hindus and Buddhists usually focus on repeating a mantra such as Aum when meditating, which is interpreted as a slow long sound. Meditation is believed to help focus the mind so that it is still. It is interesting to note that meditation and yoga seems to be a growing trend in schools as they can help children cope with modern-day stresses and encourage confidence and an enquiring mind (Barker, 2008; Ord, 2008). There are many other mantras that are used when meditating, and these can also be observed when visiting Buddhist shrines, as the monks tend to chant the scriptures or/and a mantra.

Before starting a chant, it is a good idea to have the children sitting comfortably and practise repeating a line or a word with the same intonation and diction as each other. Make sure they know when to start and stop by stating you will conduct them with hand signals because you will also be taking part in the chant and so can't speak. It's a good idea to have something they can focus on and to encourage the children to breathe from the diaphragm so that they can make a continuous sound and they do not have to stop at different times for a breath. Once they have mastered how to chant in unison you can progress to include a chant of a few parts.

To play with a chant it is best to divide the class into groups. Start with two groups and build up to as many as you feel you can. Start the first group off with a chant they are familiar with and which is at least one sentence and then once they have repeated this sentence twice introduce the next group on the second word, then the third on the third word etc. This way you should gather a selection of rhythms and providing the children are saying the mantra/sentence in the same way, then it should make an interesting sound. You could also develop this so that it is more Humanistic and non-religious and so the mantra could be the class or school motto or a code and which is personal to the children.

Playing with various tones for sounding a phrase or word such as Aum for meditation and considering how the Aum would have sounded during creation (i.e. quiet tone of Om building to loud vibrating tone) could be an interesting concept to explore with children within an RE and Music lesson. This could be another way of choral chanting so that the children start slow and quiet and build to a fast energy that is loud but not shouting, thus exploring the energy that Hindus and Buddhists believe can be created through the Aum.

National Curriculum and Non Statutory Framework links

RE =	KS1	AT2 2b, 2e
		Breadth of study 3n, 3o, 3p
	KS2	AT1 1b, 1e, 1h
		AT2 2c, 2e
		Breadth of study 3l, 3o, 3p, 3q, 3r, 3s
Music =	KS1	1a, 1c, 2b, 3a, 4d
		Breadth of study 5a, 5c, 5d
	KS2	1a, 1c, 2a, 2b, 3c, 3d, 4a, 4c,
		Breadth of study 5a, 5b, 5c, 5e

The Internet and music

As we explore in Chapter 9 there are many resources on the World Wide Web that support skills and learning within the Religious Education framework, yet surprisingly there are also some websites that can support RE and Music in a thematic and cross-curricular way. Below are a few examples of what is available and some suggestions on how you could possibly use them thematically.

Second Life

http://secondlife.com is an amazing site that contains some fantastic visual learning spaces that are similar to a 3D virtual tour; however, there is a need for caution here. Although there is a *Teen Second Life* it is for children aged 13 and over. *Second Life* is designed for adults not children. Yet I have included this site here because although it does contain adult material, I believe the technology is so amazing it will soon become available for schools.

With the development of new technologies and the already incredible places to visit on this site through a virtual person (avatar), I am certain that either the creators (Linden) will develop a learning environment for primary schools or there will be other corporations that will create similar social and learning networking sites in the near future. Either way, watch this space, as I feel *Second Life* is possibly the future for online learning.

Saying this, however, I still feel there are areas within *Second Life* that could be used with a class of children providing you are professional and ensure you control what they are doing and where they look. A fine example would be the Holocaust museum's online version of Kristallnacht with real audio accounts from survivors and various religious buildings that allow a visitor to explore their architectural features. It is important to note, however, that you never allow the children to create their own avatar or permit them to explore the site independently of an adult. The result could be that they visit areas that contain strictly adult material.

As a cross-curricular RE and Music learning environment the place Sacred Grounds – Interfaith Garden is worth a visit.

This place contains a variety of houses and areas dedicated to faiths from around the world. You can download a note card that explains some of the fundamentals of each of the faiths; however, the interesting part of this garden is the drums and bells, which are near a large bonfire and within the oriental hut.

The drums are programmed to create a certain type of beat when your avatar touches them such as 1/6 pattern or 2/6 etc. When they are chosen, the drums create a rhythm and you can watch your avatar dance or be animated so that they look as if they are creating the beat.

Logging on with three or four children each with a pre-created avatar with networked computers facilitated by an adult who is confident with this material, place an avatar/child on different drums and experiment with different beats. Listen to how they sound together and try to create a piece of music that they can perform using the interactive smart board to the rest of the class. To contextualise and extend this activity it would be useful to research into how drums and bells are used within different religions and explore why and how they are used as a form of religious worship.

Apple iTunes

Many people know about iTunes and understand that http://www.apple.com/itunes/store is an online store where you can buy digitalised music, yet it also contains music that can be downloaded free of charge. Many different types of religious music such as gospel, Christian, Islamic, Indian, classical, modern, spiritual, etc. and podcasts can be searched for on this site and then stored in an audio folder to use at a later date. I recommend that the children create their own iPod folder that contains spiritual music, which they can then discuss in future lessons where they listen to and appraise religious music either individually or as a class.

Mantras

http://www.sanskritmantra.com/simple.htm is a good website that Is effectively a music library. It contains a wealth of material, but can be used to download and explore simple mantras. This database provides explanations of the meaning of a mantra, so that children can begin to see how they are created and then possibly create and perform their own.

Hymns

http://www.hymnsite.com/ contains music to download and lyrics for hymns that can be useful to explore the interpretation of words into a musical score.

Radio

http://www.live365.com/cgi-bin/directory.cgi?genre=christian is a website that contains a selection of links to Christian radio. It would be a good idea to screen the radio stations before using them with children, as some may contain fundamentalist viewpoints that can be contrary to some parent's opinions. It might be an idea to use them as a way to look at how religious people like to use music as a way to celebrate their faith.

Other resources

If you search for religious music you will find a plethora of resources, for example www.youtube.com, but please screen them before using with children. There are some good clips of people singing in church and gospel choirs. There are also some clips associated with dance and how to interpret the religious music through worship dance.

Summary of key points

- Music has always had a close relationship with religion
- Don't let lack of knowledge about RE or Music stop you from being creative with your teaching and learning. Consider activities such as
  - Thinking books
  - Podcasts
  - Blogs
  - Song
  - Poetry

- Radio broadcasting
- Dance, drama and art
- Music and RE can be used together in schools to
  - Create and perform religious or spiritual music
  - Interpret and appraise religious or spiritual music
  - Practise religious or spiritual music
  - Develop key musical and religious skills
- There are a variety of resources available to support RE and Music. You don't need many instruments to develop Key Skills within them
- There are fantastic online resources to support RE and Music. The best are *Second Life*, any music database such as *iTunes* and The Music Manifesto website

Chapter 9
Using creative resources in Religious Education

LEARNING OBJECTIVES

In this chapter we will consider:

- The various types of resources available to help you teach RE in a creative way
- How to improve your awareness of the organisations and professionals who can support your RE teaching
- What is a creative resource?
- How to use a resource to develop creativity

It will also address elements within the following Standards:

Q6, Q7, Q14, Q15, Q20, Q25

Introduction

There are so many RE resources available in today's educational market that it can be a minefield to know which ones are the best to use. As Religious Education usually has a limited budget for resources, it is essential for you as an RE coordinator, trainee teacher or class teacher to choose key items that will support and, more importantly, enhance the lessons that you plan to teach.

This chapter will focus on how to support children's learning and development in Key Skills through creatively using

- Electronic resources
- People as a resource
- Religious artefacts and religious resources
- Paper resources

It contains four case studies that explore some of the methods of using resources.

Creative use of electronic resources

Since the implementation of the National Curriculum (NC) in 1988, the focus of Information Communication Technology (ICT) has shifted from a subject that was defined separately from the others to now where ICT is integral within the Breadth of Study of all subjects proving that there is a requirement for schools to use it (QCA, 1999:21).

There has been a natural growth towards producing electronic resources for the primary and secondary classrooms, the largest of which has been for the core subjects; however, much has been created since 2000 for the foundation subjects and RE. The following electronic resources are the tip of the iceberg of what is available and are, in my opinion, the best RE examples of what you should use to stimulate creativity in yourself and your class.

Filmed resources

Video tape is still around, but is slowly being overtaken by digital media such as DVDs, YouTube and BBC iplayer. However, many schools and suppliers still have a wealth of VHS tapes and recorders that contain snippets of good RE footage that can be valuable at the start or end of a lesson and as such should not be dismissed. When considering what to show children, it's a good idea to consider the most appropriate type of filmed footage that will help embed the RE objective of the lesson rather than the type of media it is shown through, i.e. it's not beneficial to show a 30 minute DVD if it doesn't support what you want the children to learn.

YouTube

YouTube (www.youtube.co.uk) is a controversial learning tool purely because it contains some radical viewpoints, abusive language and can encourage people to challenge traditional concepts of religion. Because of such issues, always screen a filmed clip and choose very carefully before using with KS1 and 2 children.

There are, however, some useful creative, up-to-date clips within the YouTube website, and these can be used with KS2 and possibly KS1 children. Some clips are suitable to

- Stimulate a debate about religion in the twenty-first century (KS2)
- View how religions around the world differ due to variances in culture (KS2)
- Observe religious expression such as dance and music (KS1 and 2)
- Gain information about the religion from a personal perspective (KS1 and 2)
- See religious festivals being celebrated by people who follow the faith (KS1 and 2)

Learn about Passover (http://uk.youtube.com/watch?v=Lbo8UeEddRQ) is a good example of a YouTube clip and is approximately two minutes long. It shows a typical Passover meal and briefly explains the history behind the Jewish festival. It is a valuable clip to show at the end of a unit of work to summarise the Passover celebration or as a stimulus to a lesson to try and engage the children so that they create their own YouTube clip using software such as Digital Blue Movie Creator (http://www.digitalblue.org.uk) or a camcorder about a Jewish festival or an event from a different faith. YouTube can be a useful resource for any teacher who is imaginative enough to consider different ways of using appropriate footage to stimulate creativity in the children they teach. There is a useful article by Paul Hopkins on how to use

YouTube as an RE resource in the autumn edition of *REtoday* (Hopkins, 2008) and it is worth taking a look for more ideas.

DVD and video

There are also many good DVDs that schools can buy which explore religions and have short clips suitable for the structure of a typical lesson. MCreery *et al.* (2008:31) suggest that the content of DVDs and videos is story-based or explores a specific aspect of a religion from the perspective of a child; however, I feel that this simplifies it a little, because not all filmed footage falls into these two categories. Although many suppliers such as *Articles of Faith* offer DVDs that do focus more on narrative or specifics of a living faith from a child's perspective, many other publishers are going a little further to provide resources that cover as many areas as possible. Occasionally, publishers offer DVDs and videos that contain information about culture and religion (*Good Day India*); key features of religions as a whole and not purely from the perspective of a child (*Places of Worship*) or film that stimulates discussion (*Big Questions*).

There are many types of footage that do different things and don't fit into the two simple categories suggested by McCreery *et al.* (2008), so it is up to you to consider from the variety of sources available which type of material would best suit your scheme of work and then use it effectively. Because an RE budget is low, many schools need to have an incentive when purchasing resources and so some DVDs and videos now provide a double whammy and offer another subject such as Geography or Citizenship alongside RE (*Africa's Child*) or they try to cover as much information as possible about all six major faith traditions (*Looking At Faith*) so that it encourages schools to buy what is both educationally worthwhile and cost effective. Using a DVD or video in more than one way makes it worth the money. This concept can be further explored in the spring issue of *REsource* (Constance, 2009).

So, how do you use a clip of film effectively?

It is important to consider how to use any filmed footage with children because the resource can end up being a baby-sitting tool that keeps the class quiet rather than an opportunity for learning. The best way, whether the footage is two minutes or two hours, is through chunking and embedding it within the lesson. You should use electronic footage to enhance the RE lesson and, ideally, use any filmed resource for no more than ten minutes of the lesson. It is best to use it to consolidate or extend the learning and not as a means to replace it.

Top tips for film

- Give the children questions to focus on whilst watching the clip and then discuss their answers.
- Questions should be open ended and encourage the Key Skills of reflection or thinking so ask open questions such as *Why?* or *What do you think?*
- Do something with the film after watching it in order to embed the objective of the lesson, either through discussion or an activity.
- Consider allowing the children to make their own film based on what they saw.

- Always have a purpose for the film and make sure the children know what it is, i.e. say to the children; *'We are going to do xyz with this film so make sure you focus on abc.'*
- Use a clip for approximately ten minutes in an RE lesson.

CD ROMs

CD ROM resources for schools are still selling well, and many are useful for an interactive white board at the start of a lesson. For example, *Aspects of Religion*; *Interactive Places of Worship* and *Animated Haggadah* offer facets that involve activities best suited for individual or paired work and include (embedded within the CD) photographs, PowerPoint slides and filmed footage that can be used with a KS1 or 2 class. Many publishers, however, are beginning to see the value in using their websites in addition to suppliers and, as such, there are opportunities for the content of CD ROMs such as lesson plans, activities, links to other resources, games and photographs to be individually purchased or downloaded free from the internet rather than as a whole CD ROM or textbook (http://vig.pearsoned.co.uk/catalog/main_content/0,1151,-500,00.html).

The value of this is that downloading is quick, easy to do and often less expensive because CD ROMs can, in some cases, present the problem of needing a site licence and can, therefore, only be used on a specific PC, thus restricting their use. However, CD ROMs should not be dismissed, even though they can seem pricey at times, because some contain excellent activities that can be used with many children. There are some fantastic free and purchasable resources listed on http://www.reonline.org.uk/itre/index.php that are worth reviewing for your future RE lessons.

Websites

You need to take care when viewing and using websites for Religious Education. Because a website can be created and published by anybody, it is important to consider its validity before using with children, as it may have been created for political propaganda or for the purpose of indoctrination. It is very easy to be seduced into thinking a site is ideal for RE lessons because it has an interactive story with animations, but it is essential that as a professional, you reflect on the purpose of the website and whether the information provided is appropriate and accurate.

A non-specialist in Religious Education may consider the information to be factually correct purely because it is published on the Net, but in many cases it can mislead the reader into a stereotypical or fundamentalist view of the religion. In truth, this may also happen to specialist RE teachers, as it is impossible to know everything about all aspects of every religious faction or denomination. Consequently, it is crucial that, when looking for resources and information on the Net, you keep a professional and critical eye on the content of the material and try not to be enticed by the way the site looks.

A good starting point for any information about religion or a religious resource is an established and recognised site. The University of Cumbria's website (RE-XS) is an excellent resource. Not only is it easy to navigate, but it also contains links to other well resourced and informative RE websites (http://re-xs.ucsm.ac.uk/). It is an excellent website for you to use as a source of information about RE; however, it is currently under review.

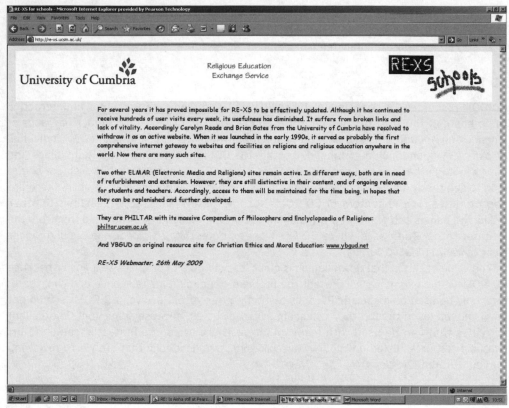

Source: http://re-xs.ucsm.ac.uk

On-line teacher resources

The following websites are useful to help you develop ideas on the ways to teach the concepts and in particular the Key Skills of RE. They either provide downloadable resources that can be adapted to suit a class or provide a nugget of an idea for you to adapt and extend to become more creative.

http://www.refuel.org.uk

http://www.bl.uk/education

http://www.curriculumonline.gov.uk/Subjects/RE/Subject.htm

http://www.teachers.tv/search/node/religious+education

http://www.reonline.org.uk/allre/tt_top.php?3x2

http://www.bbc.co.uk/schools/religion

http://www.channel4learning.com

http://www.standards.dfes.gov.uk/schemes2/religion

Case Study   **Creative use of an on-line resource**

The website **www.blewa.co.uk**, created between 2000 and 2001 when I worked at the British Library as an Education Officer and Project Manager for Words Alive!, is an example of the sort of resources available on-line. It contained a virtual area for teachers and children, which included cross-curricular Literacy resources to use in the classroom. My role was to create and pilot the activities within the site with a selection of schools and adapt them for this website.

Within this, the activity *What does it tell you?* was created to help children hone their skills at finding out information through building on knowledge they had and then forming a research question to focus on what they wanted to find out about a religion.

It required the children (in groups of about four) to look at religious images of two Hindu gods (Ganesh and Vishnu) and to answer three specific questions about the image.

1. What does it tell me?
2. What doesn't it tell me?
3. What do I want to find out?

Using the resources from the website the activity became the starting point for a project into Hinduism that used non-fiction texts to discover information about the religion. It did not require a lot of knowledge from the teacher or the children, but used religious icons as a stimulus into thinking, communication and enquiry skills. The children were not given any information about the images or faith tradition prior to the activity; this was so they could begin to consider what they already knew and begin to rationalise what they thought about aspects of the images.

The same activity, or an adapted version of it, using images from a variety of religions has been used with an assortment of ages (from 5 to 43 years) and the outcome has been that it helped adults and children take ownership of their learning about religions and become independent thinkers. They realised that they knew more about religion than they thought and they enjoyed using the web resources and this Constructivist approach to RE because it helped them consider what they didn't know about a religion thus stimulating interest and the need to discover more.

This website, along with many others, provides free downloadable images; lesson plans and ideas that can help non-specialist teachers encourage Personal Learning and Thinking Skills (PLTS) through Religious Education.

Source: Year 4 in a Church of England Primary School, Stratford, East London and http://www.blewa.co.uk

On-line children's activities

The Internet, however, is not only a teacher's directory of activities or information; it also contains a vast amount of good material that can be used with children for the purposes of learning *about* and *from* religion. The following websites can be used within RE lessons as group or independent activities or for part of the lesson through the use of an interactive white board.

Some of the examples listed below are useful for KS1 and 2 pupils and in some cases KS3.

http://www.dottieandbuzz.co.uk

http://www.blewa.co.uk/project4/children/C4_0.htm

http://www.bl.uk/onlinegallery/sacredtexts/ttpbooks.html

http://www.primaryresources.co.uk/re/re.htm

http://www.bishopsinaction.com

http://hindukids.org/index.html

http://infants.reonline.org.uk

http://juniors.reonline.org.uk

http://www.show.me.uk

http://pof.reonline.org.uk

Some of the sites offer opportunities for the children to develop skills in using the mouse; writing; communication; reflection; reading and provide lots of information about a selection of religions. Others provide examples of religious people who practise their faith on a daily basis with opportunities for the children to ask them questions about why they believe certain things, thus making the faith become more real.

On the whole, most online resources for children are

- A visual and in some cases an auditory way of putting across religious text and doctrine.
- Useful for links to virtual tours of sacred spaces.
- Child friendly information about religious practice.

- Links to religious communities.
- Chat rooms where children can ask questions about religions.

These sites are good examples of what I believe online learning should be. An electronic resource should **transform** learning, not **translate** it, and so an RE activity that uses an online or electronic source should only be used if it can't be easily recreated on paper and helps to improve the PLTS being practised within the lesson.

Virtual communities that can support RE lessons

The Internet is an amazing resource for connecting with RE communities throughout the world. The RE Directory website (http://www.theredirectory.org.uk/) that has been developed by the Culham Institute and the RE Council should be the major tool in your RE resources toolkit as it provides a list of names, numbers and addresses of hundreds of religious communities in the UK who may be of use. The database includes details of Standing Advisory Councils in Religious Education (SACRE), Local Authority Advisors and any communities in England and Wales that may offer visits or visiting speakers. It is especially useful for the non-specialist who may be undertaking an RE project about sacred places and any teacher who lives in a remote part of the country and does not have a selection of places readily available for them to visit.

The following sites are also useful as they provide information on festival dates (http://www.shapworkingparty.org.uk/) or include links to other religious communities that may be working together, have similar interests or are able to provide projects and resources that may be useful in the classroom (http://www.reonline.org.uk).

It is also important to note that Museums, Galleries and Archives can be useful communities that can provide you with resources and information about religion in the past and present. The 24 Hour Museum website is an excellent virtual database of all the museums in the UK and offers direct links to websites and exhibitions (http://www.24hourmuseum.org.uk). It also has a specially designed children's link (http://www.show.me.uk) that allows children to interactively explore some of the national treasures that are available on a variety of museum websites and which links to the National Curriculum. Unfortunately, it currently doesn't include many RE activities; however, I believe it is likely that this will change in the near future.

Although there are many ways to creatively use on-line databases to transform RE lessons, there are three main approaches.

1. To become part of a project with a real or virtual community and thus expand children's understanding of interfaith dialogue and practise the PLTS of listening and working with others.
2. To use them as databases to find people and places that can enhance learning outside and inside the classroom with guest speakers and visits.
3. To help teachers keep abreast of current trends in learning and teaching in RE and note important practice and festival dates.

On-line research in RE

In my experience as a Senior Lecturer in ITT, some trainee teachers have argued that once they are qualified it will not be necessary to know about research unless they are an RE specialist or are undertaking a Masters degree. However, I believe that knowing about current trends in education is important because it informs practice and, for anything to change for the better, the current systems need to be analysed and then new initiatives piloted.

For a change such as a framework, policy or scheme of work to be successful, it's important to understand where the change came from and understand its relevance to your own educational philosophy, this way you are more likely to accept it and use it well (Fullan, 2007). Websites and publications that explore new initiatives, legislation and ideas in Religious Education can be a useful tool because they encourage reflection on how to make RE even more successful in your school.

Research is key to developing thought and trends in educational practice and, to be a true reflective practitioner, it is essential to consider various approaches and opinions on what to teach and how best to teach RE (Pollard, 2005:61). Each of the websites suggested below offers some form of information into the current research projects that are happening in RE across the UK. Some of the projects such as The Culham Institute and The Farmington Trust offer research grants and fellowships to develop and improve RE in schools, yet all of the sites suggested here have some impact on what and how RE is taught in the UK and are fundamental to improving awareness of good RE practice.

http://betterre.reonline.org.uk/

http://www.culham.ac.uk/

http://www.farmington.ac.uk/

http://www.retoday.org.uk/index.php

http://www.natsoc.org.uk/schools/curriculum/re/

http://www.theredirectory.org.uk/journals.php

http://www.humanism.org.uk/site/cms/

http://www.faithinschools.org/

On-line information about religions

It is very easy to make mistakes and have limited knowledge about religious practice or doctrine and this is one of the reasons why RE is not taught as regularly as it should be in schools (L'Anson, 2004). The Internet can therefore be helpful in providing knowledge and can also offer advice about New Religious Movements and other world faiths that are not included in the six major faith traditions advocated by the *Non Statutory Framework for RE* (QCA, 2004). Using information and community websites (such as the examples above) to learn about lifestyle and belief systems will help you become more aware of how to support the spiritual development of the children in your class and subsequently feel more confident to teach the content of AT1 *Learning about Religion*.

The BBC website http://www.bbc.co.uk/religion is one of the best, as it is always a reliable resource. It updates its content on a regular basis and links information to general news coverage, a variety of other well established RE sites and the objectives of the National Curriculum (QCA, 1999) and *Non Statutory Framework for RE* (QCA, 2004). However, I advise you to be careful when browsing the Net for up-to-date information about religious practice and belief systems.

The problem with all websites is that they are never permanent. Many a time I have found a useful resource and then returned to the website to find it no longer working. There could be many reasons for this, but it usually happens because the domain is no longer hosting the site and so the url has changed. It could also be because the financial support of the website has ended or it has been removed by an external body due to the extremist ideologies that are represented on the site.

It is essential for you to be aware of these issues and choose resources and websites carefully. It is always worth noting the url address and the name of the organisation that created the site. This way you will be aware if the content is of a suitable nature for schools and also whether it is likely still to be available in six months' time.

When needing to gather information about a religion and its belief systems, it is much better to purchase a well researched textbook such as *Religions in the UK: A Multifaith Directory* (Fry and Weller, 1997) rather than solely using the World Wide Web for information about a religion, as you cannot rely on the website's accuracy or guarantee the democratic educational value of the content, so it is not a dependable resource. Using text-based material in tandem with the World Wide Web will mean you're less likely to make mistakes when teaching about religions.

Summary of key points

- Be creative with what you choose and how to use filmed footage
- Give children questions to focus on and discuss when watching a film
- Create your own electronic resource using Digital Blue Movie Creator (http://www.digitalblue.org.uk)
- Consider downloading some of the content of some CD ROMs from publishers' websites
- Screen religious websites carefully for inappropriate material
- Websites are useful for you to download resources, information, activities and can also offer online activities for children
- Use virtual communities to find out about how a faith is lived

Creative use of people

People are a useful resource for an RE lesson. A religion is intended to be experienced, so the best way of vicariously exploring the experience would be through other people. Children can be an excellent resource in a classroom as they are readily available to draw upon; however, this can occasionally be tiresome for the child, as they may not know the answer to the question that is asked and may also feel they do not wish to be centre of attention. Linking with religious communities and asking for a guest speaker to visit the school or for the class to visit them in their place of worship can help at such times, as they can provide a new perspective on a religious theme and assist children to begin to see how religious expression is very much part of a living faith.

However, the best way of using any guest speaker, before the visit, is to explain to the speaker in as much detail as possible what it is you want the children to learn and the structure of the visit, e.g., are they speaking about a particular topic; taking questions or conducting a lesson, etc. It is also necessary to prepare the children before the visit so that they have opportunity to create questions and are engaged in the event, understanding the purpose of the visit or visiting speaker. Filming the speaker may also be a good idea so that you can use it for future lessons and refer back to it.

The way to structure the speaker's visit can be as a

- Chat show such as *Trisha* or *Richard and Judy*.
- One-to-one interview such as a journalist on *Newsround* or the *BBC News* where the majority of the children become the non-participating audience, but have created the questions for the chosen interviewer to ask.

- Radio show (it is recorded and put onto the school website) such as Radio 4's *Any Questions?*
- Class lesson so that the speaker provides activities for the children to do and the teacher supports them.
- Hot seat where each child asks at least one question in turn and the speaker answers them.
- Presentation where the speaker talks about a given subject (possibly with PowerPoint) and the children listen, make notes then ask questions at the end.

The main purpose of a visiting speaker is to stimulate interest and learning about a religion and so it is essential that the children do something with the information gained from the speaker such as a class presentation, a filmed piece to show in assembly, posters, etc.

You as a resource

Another way of using people is when you personally experience a festival or event etc. whilst in the UK or on holiday abroad. Occasionally, it is possible to find yourself in a position where you can take snapshots of religious events such as weddings, naming ceremonies or festivals. On such occasions it is also easy to get into conversation with people about how they feel and what they are doing as the atmosphere is usually jovial and people like to mix. Such snapshots and anecdotes can be used with children to help them realise that religion is lived and that many people can experience small parts of it all over the world even if they don't practise a faith themselves. The images that you have taken with your commentary will stimulate the children's interest and show them how people participate in religious events.

| Case Study | **You as a resource** |

These snapshots were taken when I was on a study trip to Israel in 1993 as a student teacher and when I was a Global Teacher in 2004 with a charity called Link Community Development (www.lcd.org.uk).

The first photograph Is In Jerusalem. It was during Easter and people openly celebrated Palm Sunday through being involved in a procession from the Garden of Gethsemane to the Holy Sepulchre. We stumbled upon this event and I found that I was in the perfect position to take photographs of the collective expression of Christian faith. The second photographs are of a wedding in Uganda that I was lucky to be Invited to. They show that, even in an economically poor area of the world, a wedding Is a form of celebration and it is a community event.

I have used these images along with others such as my own Holy Communion picture taken around 1980 to stimulate discussion about why people take part in celebration and religious events.

I have found that the children tended to be more interested because the images were about my experiences out of the classroom. (I'm reminded here of the old adage where children think that teachers sleep in school and never use the toilet and so are shocked when they realise you go on holiday!)

They were enthralled with personal tales of the celebrations. For example: what people said to me when I asked Christians in Jerusalem how they felt about Easter; what it was like to be in such a large crowd celebrating a festival; what it felt like when I knew I was watching a procession that Jesus took just before he died on the cross; what was different about the Christian Ugandan wedding compared to UK weddings; do I still take Holy Communion; is that your mum? I was the resource in this instance.

Consequently, some children brought in their own snapshots of religious events that they had been involved with, helping to extend the class's learning about religion and a person's personal expression of religion.

When using people remember to be creative; a speaker, a child or you can be a resource but it is *how* they are used that makes them a successful and valuable tool for learning and teaching in Religious Education.

Summary of key points

- Children can be a resource but be sensitive to them being singled out
- Ensure a guest speaker knows what is expected of them
- Make sure the children have prepared questions to ask speakers
- You can be a resource
- Take photos of any religious ceremony or festival that you are involved with and use them with anecdotes in your teaching

Creative use of artefacts

There are different types of religious items readily available to buy from resource catalogues, but how to use them isn't always explained. The first thing to consider, however, is the difference between a religious resource and a religious artefact.

An artefact is an item that belongs to a religion and is used within its rituals and everyday practice, for example, a set of prayer beads, a Hindu icon of Ganesh or an Islamic prayer mat. A religious resource is an item with a religious theme, which isn't usually used as part of the everyday nature of the faith such as a story-telling doll, Christmas card or storybook. Both types of resource, however, can be used in similar ways and should be treated with respect.

Knowing how an artefact is used in a faith is crucial, so that you can use it appropriately and avoid inadvertently offending someone, for example, because Muslims wash before prayer (*Wudu*), ensure you have wet wipes handy for the children to use before handling the Qur'an so that they realise it is a special object and so should be handled with care and respect. Likewise, ensure you research into how any artefact is used in the religion it belongs to before using it with children. For example, a chalice wouldn't be placed on the floor as it is intended to contain the Communion wine, likewise an Islamic prayer mat would be put on the floor, but only if it is clean and is facing Mecca. Lack of knowledge can lead to misunderstanding and can make a teacher lose confidence and subsequently not use any artefact or produce uninteresting lessons.

Case Study

What is the artefact and how would you use it with children?

Darren Northcott, a Year 2 teacher, used artefacts as a starter to an RE lesson and the first lesson of a scheme of work. In groups of three the children had one item from a faith that they had to consider. They needed to think what the artefact or resource was and how it was used in the religion. The discussion around the item was designed to develop their curiosity and thinking skills. They discussed their answers as a group then as a class.

Darren encouraged the children to use their prior learning about religions and think about why they thought the object was a significant item. He then explained the purpose and name of each item using posters on the white board that showed how the item was used. The artefact became a springboard into research using books, resulting in a poster about the faith and a particular theme.

In this case the teacher's knowledge was invaluable to the success of the lesson. He chose to research the use of the artefacts prior to the lesson to ensure the learning and teaching was excellent.

Source: Year 2 Ellen Wilkinson Community Primary School, East London

Yet it is possible to use artefacts to audit your *own* RE knowledge and help you focus your research. Below is a case study exploring how you can improve your existing knowledge.

Case Study

What is the artefact and how would you use It to develop your own knowledge?

I have adapted the activity that Darren did with his KS1 class and used it with trainee teachers to help them recognise the gaps in their knowledge and accordingly what they needed to do to improve their understanding of the six major faith traditions so that they could confidently teach RE.

I placed a selection of artefacts (about four) from a variety of religions on each table and asked the trainees to work in groups of three to consider what each artefact or resource was, what faith it belonged to and how it might be used. They had the opportunity to quickly refer to some books and ask me for basic background information if they had none.

The trainees then had to come up with a creative way to use the artefact or resource with children in KS1 and KS2 to stimulate learning about or from religion. The outcome was that many of the trainees felt insecure about using an artefact when they didn't know its religious use. Many of them said that they had little experience in their own education with the six major faith traditions and so knew a little bit about Christianity but nothing about the other five religions. However, they did eventually came up with fantastic lesson ideas such as

- Make a poster about how to care for an artefact
- Retell the religious story using the Jewish Shofar or Moses doll
- Create their own prayer beads or mat or Kippah/Yarmulka (Jewish prayer cap) for meditation or quiet time
- Make their own mezuzah that they can put on the classroom door with their own ultimate class rule contained within it
- Create their own five items that show they belong to a community similar to the Sikh 5 Ks
- Design and make their own modern-day Nativity play

The activity with the trainee teachers became quite a good audit of their personal knowledge of religion. For many of them it became a QTS target related to Q14.

Source: Second Year Trainees, Edge Hill University, Ormskirk

I strongly recommend that you audit your knowledge so that you can assess what you know about the religions in the UK and what else you need to find out. If you use the method within this case study, you will become more confident in handling resources and teaching RE. The Personal Training Plan in Figure 9.1 that has been adapted from Copley and Priestly (1991:140) should guide you in undertaking your audit and Figure 9.2 provides you with a completed example from a final year trainee teacher so that you can see how it should be filled in.

Some things to consider when using artefacts in a classroom:

Do . . .

- Allow the children to handle the artefact and explain the various ways it is used so as to avoid stereotyping a religion, i.e. a chalice contains the actual blood of Christ in Roman Catholicism, but contains a symbolic representation of it in the Church of England.
- Use the phrase '**some** or **most** Christians, Hindus, Muslims, etc. in the UK believe...' rather than 'we' or 'all Christians' etc.
- Use a variety of artefacts of the same faith, don't limit it to one.
- Show filmed footage of how the artefact is used.
- Research into **how** and **why** the artefact is used in the faith *before* using it with children.
- Find out how many children practise a faith in your class so that they can demonstrate an artefact and you can be sympathetic to the needs of all your class including children who are non-religious.
- Always explain what they are going to do and why you want the children to re-enact a festival or rite of passage such as a wedding or naming ceremony, etc. However, make sure you adapt any ceremony so that the children and parents realise that they are not being indoctrinated into a particular faith but exploring, in their own way, how and why people take part in special religious events.
- Use the artefacts as stimuli into learning *about* and *from* the faith.

Don't ...

- Say that **every** Sikh or Hindu, etc. believes in the same thing as there are many different factions of each faith. Remember that culture has an impact on how a religion is expressed and so be aware of stereotypes.
- Say 'we think ...' unless you are teaching in a denominational school such as Roman Catholic or Church of England school as there may be children who do not have a faith and thus not everyone thinks the same.
- Put a Qur'an in a resource box or on the bottom shelf. It needs to be placed in the highest part of the room and it must be covered.
- Expect children to re-enact how to use the artefact unless they are of that religion or have volunteered to do so, e.g., do not ask them to conduct *Salat* (Islamic Prayer) unless they are Islamic or conduct Holy Communion unless they are a Christian. It is best to show a video.
- Use the artefacts as a 'show and tell' activity as it devalues and trivialises the religion.
- Worry if you don't know much about the religion. You can research what you don't know and also ask people who do practise the faith for advice.

Summary of key points

- Be aware of the difference between an artefact and a resource
- Handle artefacts respectfully and show this with the children
- Research how artefacts are used before handling them with children
- Using artefacts will make you feel more confident to teach AT1
- Audit your knowledge through looking at what you know and don't know about a religious item – use the training plans (Figures 9.1 and 9.2) to help you

Complete the sentences and fill in the boxes

Name of religion = Theme =	Name of the group of people who follow this religion = Link to QTS standard =		
In this theme I **already know...**			
In this theme I want to **find out...**			
In this theme I find >>>>> **personally challenging**			
I can >>>>> to help me **overcome the issue(s)** that challenge me			
I would like to **find more** about this theme by >>>>>	*Websites*	*Published texts*	*Asking*

Use a separate sheet to make notes on what you have discovered through further study.

Figure 9.1 Personal training plan based on self-assessment of personal knowledge

Source: Adapted from *Forms of Assessment in Religious Education: The main report form the FARE project*, FARE Project, Exeter (Copyley, T. and Priestley, J. 1991) p. 140, Reproduced by permission of the FARE project, University of Exeter School of Education and Lifelong Learning.

Name of religion = Buddhism	Name of the group of people who follow this religion = Buddhists
Theme = Rules and Regulations	Link to QTS standard =
In this theme I **already know...**	That Buddhists follow an 8 fold path and that they meditate. Not sure why. They also have something called Nirvana (I think). They have priests. Puja is worship; helps with meditation. Don't have many rules – peaceful religion – rules are mainly about being good.
In this theme I want to **find out...**	Why do they meditate if they don't have a god? Do they have any big rituals and routines? Do they have to do meditation and other rituals every day and for how long? How is the 8 fold path different from the 4 Noble Truths or are they the same? What is Nirvana? Is Karma something Hindu or Buddhist?
In this theme I find AT2 and why follow a religion **personally challenging**	I find religion challenging anyway. Buddhism I'm not so bothered about coz its peaceful and many non religious people do yoga etc and so have a pick and mix approach. Many people like the lifestyle I suppose it's a bit hippy. AT2 can be challenging. AT1 – knowledge stuff I can do coz its like anything else but AT2 is chatting about why Buddhists do things and I don't have the answer to that.
I can talk to people and do some research to help me **overcome the issue(s)** that challenge me	I could talk with people to find out why they have a religion. I usually avoid doing this coz I get a bit cross coz I don't understand why have a faith. I am agnostic I think – don't believe or disbelieve I suppose. I need to begin to see what people get out of religion before I'm confident in discussing this with kids. I could look on the www for real people and testimonials?
I would like to **find more** about this theme by looking on www, reading information about Buddhism and asking people who might know	*Websites* http://re-xs.ucsm.ac.uk www.bbc.co.uk/schools/religion www.theredirectory.org.uk look at chat rooms? – do a google search	*Published texts* McCreery, E. *et al.* (2008) *QTS Teaching RE* Weller, P. (2001) *Religions in the UK: A Multifaith Directory*	*Asking* RE Coordinator LA advisor Local Buddhist group?

Figure 9.2 Personal training plan based on self-assessment of personal knowledge; example – trainee teacher, Emma

Source: Adapted from *Forms of Assessment in Religious Education: The main report from the FARE project*, FARE Project, Exeter (Copley, T. and Priestly, J. 1991) p. 140, Reproduced by permission of the FARE project, University of Exeter School of Education and Lifelong Learning

Creative use of paper resources

Children's books

There are so many children's books that are being published at a rapid pace that I can go on forever here about excellent picture books that are not explicitly religious but can be used within RE lessons. Many have themes such as death, life, prayer, culture, which have cross-curricular or thematic links to PSHCE or Geography. They tend to relate to what the child knows already about emotions and life and so you will have a 'hook' to start a lesson with which can then be developed to explore explicitly religious issues.

- *Come Back Grandma* (Limb and Munoz) (fantastic picture book about life, death and rebirth).
- *Badger's Parting Gifts* (Varley) (*Wind in the Willows* theme about Badger dying and leaving a gift of memories).

- *Second Birth* (Radley and Richard) (addresses questions about life, birth and death).

- *Vicky Angel* (Wilson) (for older readers and is about the death of a friend and guilt of the person left behind).

- *One Child One Seed* (Cave) (a counting book that has lovely pictures to show an African culture).

- *Children Just Like Me* (Copsey and Kindersley) (looks at children's lives around the world).

- *Our Favourite Stories* (Gavin) (traditional stories from around the world).

- *Shaker Lane* (Provenson) (a community is being taken over by a company who want to flood the village. It is about change, people and belonging.)

- *The Hidden House* (Waddell and Barrett) (a house is overgrown by plants and insects and has three dolls hidden within it. Eventually a family turn the house into a home and the dolls feel they belong again. A little bit about belonging and fate.)

- *How to Live Forever* (Thompson) (amazing picture book with lots of spoonerisms. Its about a boy in search of the book with the answer of to how to live forever.)

- *The Ice Palace* (McAllister and Barrett) (a beautifully illustrated picture book about a very sick girl and the worry of her family. It explores the dreams that she has when she is in a fevered coma.)

- *Skellig* (Almond) (for older readers. An amazing book dealing with complex issues of family, belonging, life and angels. It is also now a film.)

- *A Child's Book of Prayer in Art* (Beckett) (a beautiful resource book that looks at how prayer is represented in famous pieces of art).

- *The Complete Maus* (Spiegelman) (a graphic novel suitable for KS2 and above about a survivor of the Holocaust and his experiences in Auschwitz).

- *A Christmas Card* (Theroux) (a wonderfully spiritual story full of metaphor and symbolism about a boy and his family travelling at Christmas but getting lost and staying in a mysterious cottage with a strange man and a light shown on a Christmas card that appears to move towards them).

- *The Boy in the Striped Pyjamas* (Boyne) (a simple tale about the son of a German officer befriending a Jewish boy in a Nazi concentration camp in Poland – also now a film).

- *The Silver Sword* (Serraillier) (a thought provoking modern classic about a group of Polish refugee children surviving World War II and the aftermath thereof).

There are also fantastic storybooks about festivals and in particular Christmas. It is wonderful to teach the Christmas story from a different perspective. The following texts are some that I have discovered over the years and have used with children so that they could write their own Christmas story from a perspective of their choosing. It's a great way of encouraging creativity and also understanding the messages of the Christmas story. I have seen some teachers use a few of the following stories as an alternative to the traditional Nativity play at Christmas or have used a different book with each year group so that the children were able to extend their understanding of what the impact of the birth of Christ would have been.

- *Granny goes to Bethlehem* (Weston) (where was Mary's mum in the traditional tale? This shows a modern twist of the story. For young children.)

- *The Witness* (Westell) (a beautiful book about a pregnant cat in Jesus' stable).

- *A Night the Stars Danced for Joy* (Hartman) (from the perspective of the shepherds. A beautifully illustrated book.)

- *This is the Star* (Dunbar and Blythe) (perspective of the wise men. Beautiful illustrations.)
- *The Nativity Play* (Butterworth and Inkpen) (a funny take on the primary school Nativity play.)
- *The First Christmas* (Pienkowski) (using original text from the New Testament this book uses shadow puppet illustrations to explore the story.)
- *Jesus' Christmas Party* (Allan) (from the perspective of the innkeeper. Very funny and lovely illustrations.)

These books are excellent because they contain amazing illustrations and lots of opportunities for discussion and reflection. There aren't many texts available about the different perspectives of other Christian festivals or religions, so Christmas is an excellent one to develop, as it is something every primary school tends to address each year and there is usually a fantastic new book published every other year.

There are some books, however, that explicitly explore Religion and can be used in English and/or RE lessons for the development of research skills or help with understanding religious events in history and sacred texts. Some good examples are *Eyewitness Guides: Religion; Look and Wonder Gods and Goddesses* (Morley, 1998); *Religions of the World* (Lambert, 1993) and *The Complete Maus* (Spiegelman, 2003), which is an amazing graphic novel about the Holocaust, where the Nazis are cats and the Jews mice and would be suitable for upper Key Stage 2 and Key Stage 3. Using original child-friendly sacred texts such as *A Child's First Bible* and *The Manga Bible* (www.themangabible.co.uk) (Siku, 2007) (the latter is another graphic novel that adapts the text of the Old and New Testaments and interprets the religious stories in a creative way with a modern look and twist) can also remind children that stories tend to be at the heart of a faith and can be interpreted in a variety of creative ways.

You might also want to use texts such as these to help develop your own knowledge base so that you become more confident when teaching the stories and doctrine of the faith. Sometimes, having things explained simply can help a non-specialist understand the basics of the religion so that they eventually feel more confident to develop onto reading the more technical versions.

Teacher's books

There are some teacher-specific, text-based resources that can be bought to support RE lessons. The *Teaching RE* series, created by the Christian Education Movement (CEM) (e.g. *Teaching RE: Sikhism* CEM, 1994), are excellent as they explore each of the major faith traditions in turn and provide a teacher with valuable information and lesson ideas to use with various aged classes. In addition, Channel 4 Learning provides resource materials such as stories, activity ideas and general information that support their TV programmes and websites, i.e. *Stop, Look, Listen Dottie and Buzz* (www.dottieandbuzz.co.uk) (Lazenby, 1999) and the *Animated Tales of the World* series (Malcolm, 2000). Some teacher-based resources are useful for ideas and general lesson content and can, on occasion, provide worksheets or pupil workbooks, although caution is needed when using such materials.

Death by worksheet!

It is very tempting to use worksheets when you are not sure of a subject, but it is essential to consider whether they are necessary. To encourage creativity, a child needs to be permitted to express their learning in a way that suits them (see Chapter 1). Worksheets can, by their design, encourage differentiation by ability rather than outcome and the learning is presented through a clearly defined design. Worksheets stifle creativity, because they have an expected result and because of this, should be avoided.

I do, however, acknowledge that there is a need for a published scheme of work or set of lesson plans with worksheets for some teachers either because they lack confidence or are very busy, yet I stress they should be used with caution. If you need to use a worksheet ensure it is designed to encourage high-order thinking skills and isn't simply a colouring-in or retelling activity.

A good worksheet should provide a scaffold for the children to demonstrate what they know, while offering the opportunity for children to express their personal opinions and practise Personal Learning and Thinking Skills (PLTS) such as enquiry and reflection. Margaret Cooling's *Jesus Through Art* (1999), *The Bible Through Art* (2000) and *Assemblies from the Gallery* (2006) contain fantastic ideas for classroom RE lessons and collective worship ideas. They include some worksheets which, on the whole, are useful because they provide a stimulus for thinking and are not prescribed. Another good example of worksheet type activity is the *Biblos* Curriculum Resources series edited by Terence Copley. These are a set of pupil workbooks, published by the Religious and Moral Education Press, and are good for enabling the children to talk and reflect on issues related to destiny or encounter, etc. and relate to stories within the Christian Bible. The final example, however, is *Ready Resources Religious Education* resource booklets (Book 1 and 2) by Lynne Broadbent which are useful because they contain CDs that can be used with an interactive whiteboard and contain lesson ideas. These resources do not restrict a child's or a teacher's creativity and encourage PLTS and, consequently, are suitable for RE lessons.

When looking for a worksheet or pupil book for children to work with my advice is, before you use it with them, professionally criticise it; ask yourself what learning will happen through it and how it will encourage the children's personal and academic development in RE? If your responses are positive then use it, otherwise make one yourself or better still, don't use a worksheet: Be more creative!

Summary of key points

- There are numerous implicitly religious books available in book shops that are fantastic for RE lessons
- Many picture books have excellent themes that link well with RE
- Christmas can be presented from different perspectives using an array of excellent picture books
- Consider using graphic novels to stimulate creativity
- Teacher books offer ideas and advice on how to teach RE and contain some good activity ideas
- Avoid worksheets, because they stifle creativity.

Where can I get creative resources?

There are many educational suppliers that offer artefacts and opportunities to buy materials to support RE lessons, although *Articles of Faith* are the main suppliers, with their own catalogue, http://www.articlesoffaith.co.uk/, and who also supply other educational traders. As previously mentioned, REonline has a fantastic overview of what resources are available and TeachersTV offers a programme called *Resource Review* that occasionally shows what is available on the RE market (http://www.teachers.tv/video/3017).

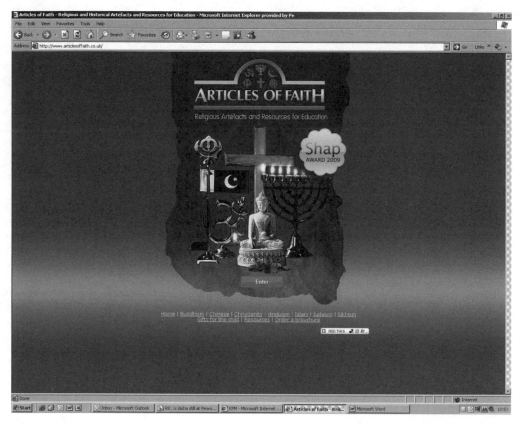

Source: www.articlesoffaith.co.uk

Alternatively, you can look to the local religious community and ask parents, congregations and leaders from places of worship if they have any clothes or religious items that they can donate to school. It is surprising what you will be offered. Likewise, raid your cupboards! Many people have a christening certificate, advent candle, Christening robe, photographs of festivals, a sari, an icon or rosary beads hidden away that you might want to use in some form with children.

Summary of key points

Ten top resource tips

Whatever you choose or wherever you obtain your RE resources, here are ten top tips in no particular order to consider when planning to use them:

1. Choose filmed footage carefully, especially if downloading from a website such as YouTube

2. Use established and recognised websites when trying to gather information about a religion

3. Use any filmed footage for no more than 10 minutes in a lesson, ideally at the start or in the conclusion to stimulate or consolidate learning

4. Only choose electronic activities that will transform and not translate learning in RE, e.g., if you can reproduce the activity using a paper and pencil then don't use the electronic resource, as its only educational value is a visual stimulus rather than a pedagogical tool

5. Prepare the children before a guest speaker arrives so that they have a question each and can use the opportunity to its best advantage

6. Avoid worksheets, especially if they are using low order thinking skills

7. Use opportunities such as holidays, family events, christenings or weddings to gather filmed footage or photographs that can be used in school to enhance learning

8. Ask local communities for any religious clothing or items that they are replenishing, and so may not need anymore, and raid your own cupboards for any religious items such as a rosary, Eid card, Christmas card, sari or advent candle that you can use in school

9. Use resources that will enhance an RE lesson and help to develop the Personal Learning and Thinking Skills such as communication skills, reflective skills, thinking skills and enquiry skills

10. Use children as a resource – they will know lots about how they live with or without a religion and will be able to explain it to others through a variety of creative methods.

Chapter 10
Planning for creative Religious Education

LEARNING OBJECTIVES

In this chapter we will consider:

- The purpose of planning
- How to create an RE medium-term plan
- How to create a cross-curricular/thematic lesson plan
- Differentiation in RE

It will also address elements within the following Standards:

Q3a, Q3b, Q10, Q19, Q20, Q22

Introduction

This chapter will help you gain an understanding of how to create medium-term and short-term plans that encourage Personal Learning and Thinking Skills (PLTS) in RE.

Creative planning

Kyriacou (1998) suggests that planning has five purposes that help a teacher focus on what they are teaching and why they are using the activities they have chosen. However, although I agree with the principles that he lists, I feel that planning can be more focused and have a threefold purpose:

1. For the class teacher, teaching assistant or supply teacher to know what they are teaching.

2. To ensure children's learning progresses and that the teaching is age appropriate.

3. To have a record of the teaching that has occurred throughout a child's education for accountability to the stakeholders such as the children, the school, the parents and Ofsted.

Once a teacher is aware of these purposes, they should begin to see that their planning is not only an important document for them personally, on a practical day-to-day level, but is also a public record and as such should be detailed and clear to follow.

Types of planning

Planning is a bit like a Russian matryoshka doll. Each plan nests within the other; making sure that there is progression, the legal requirements of the subject are covered and that children learn creatively.

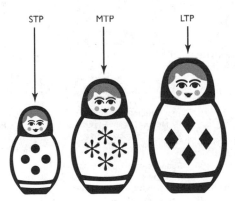

Long-term (LTP) is the largest of the planning formats and is a broad overview of what a child should learn within a full year or within a Key Stage; the National Curriculum and the *Non Statutory Framework for Religious Education* (QCA, 2004) are examples of long-term plans. Medium-term (MTP) is the next stage and fits into the long-term plan. It uses the objectives outlined for a specific year group and loosely defines what should be taught at different times of the year. It contains broad details of some of the content of the lessons and the type of activities that could be covered on a session-by-session or week-by-week schedule. A Local Authority RE scheme of work is an example of a medium-term plan. Short-term (STP) is the smallest, but the most detailed and specific plan. It is either weekly or daily and includes detail of what activities will be in the lesson, the various resources needed, lists of new vocabulary that needs to be addressed and differentiation. The objectives are taken from the MTP.

There are so many different types of planning formats that it is difficult to know which is the best to use, but whatever the format, the best advice would be to choose a style that makes sense to you and then adapt it to suit your needs. There are many textbooks that provide good examples and explore how to plan appropriate lessons: Jacques and Hyland (2000); Hoodless *et al.* (2003); and McCreery *et al.* (2008) provide good examples of RE plans and explain the planning process. They are worth reading for further information, along with some key websites that publish schemes of work such as REonline and RE-XS.

Creating medium-term plans for RE

For a creative curriculum it is a good idea to decide how to organise what needs to be taught, so that you can put them into some general order that builds on the children's skills and knowledge. Evans-Lowndes (1991:2) suggests that the best way to start to organise the content of RE would be to create a topic plan occasionally called a topic web, thematic map or themed plan. This is where the objectives of RE (taken from the Local Authority syllabus) are collected into a theme and the content is mapped around it. The process of creating a themed plan can help you clarify what needs to be taught and what sort of activities you could do to meet the learning objectives (Figure 10.1). The ideas of the plan are then numbered so that there is an order to the activities and each lesson builds on previous skills and knowledge (Figure 10.1).

What is a sacred space? 1
Activity = explain that religions have special places and we are looking at 2 religious places (synagogue and church) to get an idea why sacred spaces are important. Explain they will have a speaker and visit to a synagogue. They try to come up with 2 questions to ask the speaker whilst drawing a place that is special to them.

Christian Church 4
Activity = Virtual tour of a church
Look at the features of it
Compare to the features of the synagogue – How are they used?
Watch *Dotty and Buzz video*

Sacred Space 8
What would an ideal place of peace look and feel like? Design a place for the home corner – best design gets to make it and the class use it

Sacred Space – What should a sacred space look like? 7
Activity – discuss how religious people look after a place that is special to them. Compare the 2 religions we have looked at and find similarities on how they are looked after.
Write/draw visual instructions on how to look after a sacred space – no matter what religion.

SACRED SPACE
Year 1
Religious Education
Medium Term Planning
Themed Plan

Resources: art paper, pastels, video of synagogue, question cards/thought bubbles, permission letters for visit, pictures of church, labels for church, music, design brief, www, Dotty and Buzz video

Jewish Synagogue 2
Activity = Look at video of what happens in a synagogue
Guest speaker to explain
Children ask questions into why the synagogue is special and why Jews use it in the way they do

Christian Church 6
Activity = why is it important to have a place of worship? Why are there so many different types of church buildings? Link to pictures and previous lessons
What do they think a Christian church should look like on the outside and inside and why?
Present their designs ideas to the class in any way they want to

Jewish Synagogue 3
Activity = visit a synagogue
Look at the religious art and layout of the synagogue. What makes it look and feel special?

Christian Church 5
What happens in a church?
Drama and role play various Christian celebrations – link with *Dotty and Buzz* video

Figure 10.1 Themed plan for Year 1

Belle Wallace (2001) takes this idea further and develops a themed plan with a skills-based approach as the focus to the sessions rather than an activity. Wallace considers how to develop thinking skills within a subject and has created a rubric that scaffolds the process of thinking (2001:49, 114-17). It originated from earlier work where children's problem solving abilities were encouraged through Active Thinking in a Social Context within a concept called a TASC wheel (Wallace and Adams 1993). Wallace's plan considers the skills of problem solving and thinking through dynamic headings (2001: 14-15). Figure 10.2 is an example of how to adapt and use Wallace's TASC wheel to develop a themed plan for Religious Education.

Hoodless *et al.* (2003:37), however, use the analogy of a tree to explain how to organise planning. They state that understanding the stages of the planning process, including the use of assessment, happens before creating the lesson activities, because knowing how the different documentations feed into each other is important in ensuring successful learning experiences (2008:36). Hence the MTPs (occasionally called unit plans) are the branches that connect to the trunk (which represents the long-term plan, i.e. the National Curriculum) and the trunk links to roots (that symbolise the Education Acts, etc). The teacher is unable to create individual lesson activities without the branches, trunk and roots. This means that, unlike the themed plans of Figures 10.1 and 10.2, the objectives of the MTP come before the lesson ideas.

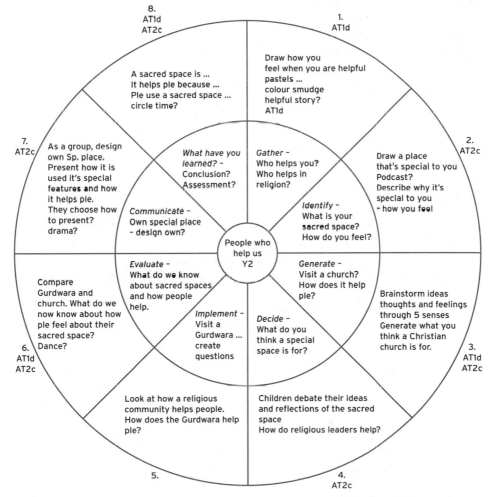

Figure 10.2 A trainee teacher's example of adapting the concept of the Belle Wallace TASC wheel (2001) to inform medium-term planning

Source: adapted from *Teaching Thinking Skills Across the Primary School*, David Fulton Publishers (B. Wallace 2001) Routledge (UK) (part of Taylor & Francis)/Cengage/Thomson

It is difficult to create any lesson activity without acknowledging the interrelation of the documentation that feeds into it, but starting the planning process by creating a themed plan can be a useful tool to help you gather ideas and aid you in beginning to see progression within the subject. Thus, I suggest you use all of the aforementioned approaches to help you create a scheme of work.

How to write a medium-term plan for RE

Start with a long-term plan such as the Local Authority syllabus or the *Non Statutory Framework for Religious Education* (QCA, 2004): what do they want you to teach? Look at the programmes of study and if they are broad, break them down into two or three clear statements and try to consider a theme such as sacred spaces or religious stories that can connect the ideas.

Case Study — **Creating a medium-term plan**

Stage 1 of the process

Non Statutory Framework for Religious Education (QCA, 2004)

> *KS1 At1 1d*
> *Pupils should be taught to:*
> *Explore how religious beliefs and ideas can be expressed through the arts and communicate their responses*
>
> *KS1 AT2 2c*
> *Pupils should be taught to:*
> *Identify what matters to them and others, including those with religious commitments, and communicate their responses*

Jane (not her real name), a Year 2 student at Edge Hill University, looked at the programmes of study (POS) from the Non Statutory Framework for RE. She realised that there were too many to choose from and was concerned with how to indentify which one to use. She decided to see if any of them matched the class topic of *People who Help Us* and, with the support of the RE coordinator, she reflected on the children's prior learning and chose one POS from AT1 and one from AT2 that seemed to be most suitable to the class topic. She then translated them into simpler sentences so that they could become the learning aims for a unit of work; making sure that they were not too broad.

> *AT1 1d = the children will . . .*
> *Consider how people show how they feel about their religion*
> *Look at the art in sacred spaces to see how people feel about their religion*
> *Explore how a sacred space is used*
>
> *AT2 2c = the children will . . .*
> *Explore through art, discussion, drama why a sacred space is important*
> *Explain through art, discussion, drama what they think about places that are special to themselves and others*

The learning aims became the focus for what Jane was going to try to achieve through the activities.

Stage 2 of the process

Jane then made a mind map using the adapted Belle Wallace's TASC wheel (2001) to collect her first thoughts about the objectives (see Figure 10.2) and added specific activity suggestions to the general ideas so that they were a little more detailed.

Stage 3 of the process

Finally, she reconsidered the order in which she wanted to do the activities, so that they built on communication and thinking skills and also developed RE knowledge to include any resources that might be useful.

Stage 4 of the process

This themed plan was then translated into a medium-term plan (MTP) also known as a scheme of work (SOW) where the learning objectives from the programmes of study and the Key Skills were included (see Figure 10.3). The MTP includes the ideas from the themed plan and is placed into a distinct format so that it is clear to follow and provided a definite structure for the lesson.

Non Stat Links:	Objectives	Activity	Key Skills
AT1d, AT2c Year 2 Summer Term 2nd Half	Links thematically to the Geography curriculum and in a cross-curricular way to PE, Art, ICT and English (See MTP)	**Language Focus:** sacred, space, religion, community, adjectives, feel, emotions **Resources:** Podcast software, pastels, paper, digital cameras, music, PE scheme of work, parent letters for visits, large paper for posters, list of key websites	**Prior Learning:** Children have looked at Religious Leaders and Religious Journeys in Christianity and Islam. They have built on PLTs in other lessons
Session 1	**Gather** ideas on what is sacred Chn will explore why a place is special and what makes it special	What is a sacred space? How do you feel in a sacred space? How do you treat people in a special place? How do you feel in a place that is special? List describing words for your special place and the people who may share that space with you. Describe onto a Podcast a place that is special and why it is special – put onto the school website to explain that this is our RE topic for this half term (see ICT MTP)	Gather ideas about special places Communication with talk partners Describing words and phrases Podcast – ICT skills
Session 2	Chn will **Identify** how people show how they feel about their religion Identify how they feel when they help others	Who helps you? Who helps in a sacred space? Why do they help? Who helps in religions? Using pastels produce art that shows how you feel when you are helpful . . . choose colours and it can be any design – it is about how they FEEL Once they have completed their picture, discuss their choice of colours, the technique they used with the pastels and their design once they have completed (see Art MTP) Link the theme of helping others to Jesus' Great Commandment of loving others and being role models	Identify how they feel when they are helpful or when someone is helpful to them Use pastels appropriately Visually and verbally express emotions

Session 3	Chn will **generate** ideas on how people show that their religion is important to them Thematic link to Geography	Visit a church. Look at the art in the building and the things that people do...what do they tell you about how people feel about Christianity? Answer this through their 5 senses – touch, taste, smell, see, hear (link and develop into feel) Make a mind map that shows the thoughts they had about how people use the church when they focused on their senses Make a senses poster as a group whilst in the church demonstrating how the church is used and why people use it. How does the 'church' help people?	Look and reflect Question Use their senses Reflection on how church has 2 meanings
Session 4	Chn will **implement** the theory from previous session to see if they are correct in why a sacred space is important	Debate – what is a sacred space for? Children use key websites that help them look at other sacred spaces (religious and non-religious) and they then work as a group to come up with a presentation that answers the question They can choose any way they wish to present their ideas – drama, music, art, ICT etc., but they need to have evidence to show how they came to their conclusion	Communication ICT Teamwork
Session 5	Chn will **decide** why they think a sacred space is important Thematic link to Geography	Visit a gurdwara and look at why and how it is used and to see why it is important to Sikhs. How do Sikhs help people? Using digital cameras the children will collect visual representations of their ideas about how people use a sacred space and how Sikhs help others and place them with notes into their thinking books	Look Question Listen
Session 6	Chn will **evaluate** why think places and people are important	What do we now know about both sacred spaces and our own spaces? Evaluate the commonality Create a class dance/group dance about how people use a sacred space, how it makes them feel, why use it and how it and the people who use it can help others (see PE MTP). Evaluate in this session what they know about sacred spaces and make a list of adjectives to describe how it is used and how people feel about it. They then turn the adjectives into movement	Communication through the body of how people feel and what people do in a sacred space PE objectives
Session 7	Chn will **learn** from experience What have the children learned about how people help us?	Children reflect on their term's topic and privately reflect on and complete the following statements • A sacred space to me is... • A sacred space to someone who has a faith is ... • A sacred space can help people because... • People use sacred spaces to... They then share their thoughts during a focused circle time	

Figure 10.3 MTP Jane: 'People who help us' – medium-term plan or scheme of work
Source: Year 2 class in a Primary School, Telford, Shropshire.

Every school has their own format for medium-term planning, so Jane's example in Figure 10.3 is not the only way to represent one. An MTP for RE is usually half a term's work; this would be 5 to 7 lessons each lasting approximately 1 hour. A Roman Catholic (RC) school, however, has more hours dedicated to Religious Education (as it is considered a core subject) and has published schemes of work that RC schools are encouraged to follow. They are called *Here I Am* or *The Way, the Truth and the Life* and provide a selection of lesson plans to develop knowledge and understanding of Catholicism (CTS, 2002). They are based on the Catechism of the RC Church and prescribe what should be taught and how to teach an objective on a week-by-week basis. It is, however, still advisable to adapt the activities to encourage creativity if you feel they do not develop PLTS in both AT1 and AT2 to a suitable degree.

With every medium-term plan or syllabus that is given to you, it is important, as a professional, to reflect on what is the best approach to teach the identified learning objective and then adapt the content to suit your teaching style and the personalities of your class. This can be done through annotating the activities so that there is a record of how you will adapt them or rewriting the activities, but keeping the original objective as suggested by Webster *et al.* (2009:1).

Thematic and cross-curricular medium-term planning

As discussed in Chapter 4, there is a slight distinction between thematic and cross-curricular teaching, yet both approaches are useful for developing creative learning. There are various ways of planning for cross-curricular and thematic learning and so again, it is best to find the style that makes the most sense to you and your school.

An RE MTP that is cross-curricular usually has references to a plan from a different subject. It can be written so that two subjects are planned together and delivered at the same time (see Figure 10.4) or It can be planned with the one subject in mind and a reference to the other subject's medium-term plan (see Figure 10.3). Neither is wrong; the style you decide to use depends on your timetable and whether you want to teach in a purely cross-curricular way or whether you want a more subject-based approach, but when there is a natural opportunity to marry the objectives of RE with another subject then you teach the subjects simultaneously within one lesson.

NC Links Art:	Objectives	Activity	Key Skills
1b, 2a, 2c, 3a, 4a, 4b, 5a, 5b, 5c **Spring Term** **Non Stat Links:** 1c, 1f, 1g, 1h, 2c, 3a, 3b, 3d, 3f, 3i, 3k, 3q, 3r	**Cross-curricular RE with Art** Extending learning to develop skills with AT2 learning from religion and use/manipulate non traditional art materials	**Language Focus:** Emotional language to do with feelings and description. Nirvana, Buddhism, 5 Pillars, Salat, Zakat, morality **Resources:** Non-fiction texts, www Various colours of plasticine, acetate and pens, blu-tack, smashed tiles, grout, paving slabs, safety goggles and gloves, aprons, funding for lavender and tiles (ask local hardware business to be partners and donate?)	**Prior Learning:** **Art** – chn have used a variety of traditional media and are familiar with the design and evaluation process **RE** – chn have visited many religious sites and have reflected on the various ways people express their faith
Session 1	The chn will **Gather** thoughts on what rules mean to them on a personal basis and within Christianity Use acetate pens to produce a visual metaphor of a 'rule' or code that they live by – develop skills in mark making	Discuss the various rules in school, football matches, shopping malls, etc. Why are they there? Talk partners list what they know about rules in society and why we have them and feedback in class discussion Moral rules – do we have any? List them as a class/group Religious rules – what do you know? Brainstorm ideas Look at the Christian and Jewish 10 Commandments and the New Testament Great Commandment – why do you think they were created? Are they still necessary today? Create a personal code/slogan that sums up a personal code or rule that they follow e.g.' Live life to the full!' Produce a piece of window art using acetate pens that symbolises their code – put onto the class window	Verbal communication Team work Reflection Listening skills Design a visual metaphor Use of colour mixing Mark making to produce block colour on a difficult surface

NC Links Art:	Objectives	Activity	Key Skills
Session 2	Chn will **identify** the purpose and importance of the 5 pillars of Islam Design and create a sculpture that shows what they think the pillars mean to Muslims	Using a selection of non-fiction texts and websites the children will work in pairs to identify the 5 Pillars of Islam. Share what they have discovered as a class then discuss – Why they are called pillars? Why are there Five Pillars not three or ten? What do they know about the importance of the pillars to a Muslim – ask any chn in class who are members of the Islamic faith for their perspective – use prior learning from year 3/4 to build on reflection skills Using plasticine the children produce a piece of art that visually represents the importance of the Five Pillars to the faith and how they keep the faith together. They can mix colours if they wish and manipulate materials with tools and different parts of their hands/fingers/thumb to produce the sculpture	Reflect on prior knowledge Explain Use emotional and religious vocabulary Have an opinion Manipulate plasticine to produce a piece of art
Session 3 & 4 (2 lessons)	**Generate** a school stepping stone area for the school garden that represents Eight Steps to happiness And **implement** their ideas to Create a mosaic for outdoor art display	The children look at the Buddhist Eightfold Path Discuss what it means and then ask them to create their own Eight Steps to Happiness. Share with each other in a circle time and ask why they are their steps As a class decide on a class set of 8 steps to happiness in school and then using paving stones/slabs, the children in groups produce mosaic representation of one of the steps (using outdoor masonry paint, smashed tiles and grout) HEALTH AND SAFETY CHECK NEEDED When ready, the Eight Steps are then placed in the vegetable and flower beds of the school garden so that they create a path through them. Would be good to plan lavender amongst them – ask HT	Reflect on what makes them happy Team work Verbal communication Use grout and jigsaw mismatched tiles to create a mosaic

Figure 10.4 Cross-curricular MTP: RE and Art. Theme: Rules and regulations (extract from MTP), Year 5/6 (2 hours per lesson)

How to write a short-term plan for RE

A short-term plan takes the MTP a step further and now adds more detail. If you consider Hoodless *et al.*'s (2003:37) analogy of a tree then the MTP is the branch, and the STP is the apple that grows from it. The main thing to focus on in a STP, however, is what you want the children to *know, understand* and *do* within the lesson; this is where you need to make sure that the objective isn't too broad and that when you are sharing it with the children, you ensure it uses language that they can understand.

Most teachers divide a lesson into three parts; beginning, middle and end. The 'Beginning' is usually where the lesson objective is introduced to the children using child-friendly language. In this section, start finding out what the children already know and introduce what you want them to know next. The next stage of the lesson is 'Understand' and 'Do' and is usually the middle part of the lesson. The middle section is trying to get the children to understand a concept, usually through an activity of some sort. The third and final part of the lesson is the 'Conclusion', which is where you consolidate or reinforce what they have learnt and then direct them towards the next lesson and the next concept to learn. The conclusion, which is also called the 'Plenary', is not a time for explaining what everyone did and showing work (although this has its merits at times) but should be used as a learning opportunity.

Some teachers, however, extend the lesson so that it has more than three parts. They break the learning into chunks, which then makes for a fast-paced lesson that can have an introduction, three or four activities and a conclusion. Wallace's TASC wheel (2001) is a good way to consider how to structure your lesson, especially if you wish to ensure you take a thinking skills approach to the learning. Figure 10.5 demonstrates how to structure the lesson using specific headings that develop reflection and problem solving in RE.

Lesson 2 of 6	Objectives taken from the RC Scheme of Work	Language	Resources
Year 3 & 4 mixed classes	**AT1** Know Jesus' teaching on sorrow and forgiveness Know that Jesus called people to change and turn away from sin to receive the love of God **AT2** Deepen awareness of forgiveness **Art** Be able to express personal thought through art Manipulate paint to explore colour mixing Use tools appropriately	Forgiveness Big and little questions Sin Symbols Design Image Emotional language Mix/blend Thin/thick brush stroke	Paint Paper *Finding Nemo* dvd Images from last week Paintbrushes Pots Water Aprons Big paper I wonder paper 5 Ws as prompts
Introduction **Gather** ideas	Explain the difference between big and little questions – what they are. Relating to making to the poor/good choices from last week ask if anyone can think of a what, where, who, when, why or how question about making choices Use a painting that portrays 'forgiveness'. What 'big' questions do they have about the image? Write questions on the flipchart	**Differentiation** G, S & Out Mixed ability talk partners to help think of a question Levelled questions directed to specific chn (TA with pupil X)	**Assessment Focus** Look to see if they are thinking for themselves or simply reflecting what they think the teacher wants to hear
Activity 1 **Identify** and then **generate** understanding	Recap *Finding Nemo* from last week and how he disobeyed his father – look at new clip of how Nemo's father forgave him for making a poor choice and turning away from his teaching IN TALK PARTNERS consider How do you think Nemo felt when his Dad forgave him? How do you think Nemo's dad felt when Nemo asked for forgiveness and was sorry for disobeying him? **Teaching point:** Relate the clip and the image of forgiveness to their relationship with God – how occasionally Roman Catholics turn from God and make poor choices that God isn't happy with . . . relate to film and discuss how forgiveness was still given when Nemo asked for it and was sorry	**Differentiation** G, S & Out Mixed ability talk partners Prompts to help thinking – TN to support with directing chn towards prompts	**Assessment Focus** Are they aware of how making a poor choice is deciding to disobey God?

Art and RE Activity 2 & 3	Activity 2 – 10 minutes but is also throughout activity 3	Differentiation G, S & Out	Assessment Focus
Decide on image and a big question	They need to think of a puzzling question in pairs that they want to openly raise about forgiveness that uses any of the 5 Ws or how . . . write it on a thought bubble that says I wonder The children consider I wonder ... Why forgiveness is important, etc. If can't think of a q that's ok	Mixed ability pairs – less confident writer is scribe, more confident writer helps with spelling TA to support with prompts and may scribe if some chn stuck	What do the questions show about how they are thinking about forgiveness? Do they come up with the word Sin? Are the qs in any way related to the Roman Catholic message of turning away from God?
Implement idea for painting	**Activity 3 – using paint** Explain the art activity (DO NOT PROVIDE AN EXAMPLE). They need to think of a symbol/ design/image that represents what forgiveness is to them personally. They will then paint that symbol using the primary colours available. It can be anything they wish – doesn't have to be a picture **Teaching point:** Encourage colour mixing – demonstrate to recap if necessary Remind them of skill of holding a brush and choosing the right sort of brush for different techniques and style	Support with colour mixing and use of tools	Are they aware of what it feels like to forgive and be forgiven?
Plenary Evaluate and communicate	If anyone wishes, share two examples of the children's symbols and explore their meanings and then look at some of the 'I wonder' questions . . . explain that we will try and revisit these as the weeks go by and also in a display In pair/share partners, they need to think of and write a definition of what forgiveness is Share a few then relate to the Catechism definition of forgiveness	Differentiation Out, Org & G Ask for volunteers yet show the examples that are the most expressive and creative Mixed ability talk partners	Assessment Focus What does the definition say about their understanding of the RC view of forgiveness? Are they able to verbally and pictorially communicate their view of forgiveness? Have they been able to explore their ideas through art?
Evaluation of the lesson and future learning – What have they learnt? What needs to be planned for next?	ART RE		Objectives for next lesson . . .

Figure 10.5 Cross-curricular short-term plan for extended lesson of more than three parts for Year 3/4

Source: From a case study of cross-curricular planning with the RC scheme of work – *The Way, the Truth and the Life* – undertaken at an RC primary school in Preston, Lancashire

There are other models for planning such as the Field of Enquiry Model promoted in the Lancashire Agreed Syllabus for RE (Lancashire SACRE, 2006) and further explored in Webster *et al.* (2009) where two case studies suggest starting a lesson with a shared human experience. However, whatever approach you decide to take for planning there are, I believe, two essential ingredients that you must consider in every one: Assessment and Differentiation. Assessment will be discussed in more detail in Chapter 11, but differentiation is an important factor for personalised learning.

Differentiation

In my experience, trainee teachers generally seem to consider differentiation to be about providing different tasks and activities for various groups of children. I have noticed when I have visited schools or looked through assignments, that the RE activities within the plans tend to be mainly based on writing, e.g., a letter, story or recount, so the differentiation is about supporting a child's writing within a genre rather than the child's understanding of religion or a religious concept. Hence the learning for children who find writing difficult can be reduced as the task becomes a barrier to accessing creativity and understanding.

To me, this view of differentiation is too narrow and provides limited learning opportunities. To develop PLTS, we need to think creatively about differentiation and that means dividing your class into groups that suit the activity that has been planned and support the children's learning in Religious Education. So when planning, using a mnemonic such as GOTOS can help you remember that there is a selection of differentiation methods (not just one) that may be suitable for your class.

Groupings – choose the best sort of group to support learning, e.g., talk partners, mixed ability pairs, mixed ability threes or groups, ability groups or pairs, snowballing into a group, friendship groups or expert groups, etc.

Organisation – how to organise your classroom. A child who has behaviour issues may need to be near an adult or you might need to change the classroom around to advocate a debate or large art work, etc. Make the classroom environment a form of differentiation so that it doesn't become a barrier to creativity and learning.

Task – differentiation by task. This means a task/activity is planned to suit a specific need for a specific child or group of children, e.g., coloured paper for a dyslexic child or a specific writing tool for a physical need that a child may have or the use of visual aids, etc. for a child with visual learning needs. This may mean you have six different activities that cater for the various needs within the class. Occasionally some needs and abilities are grouped together but don't assume that there are always three or four different abilities in a class. There are usually more specific needs that should be considered and catered for.

Outcome – this is where the children have the same activity, but can complete it to their own level of competency. The outcome is different for each child, but the task is the same.

Staff – a member of staff is designated to support a particular child or group of children. You must say, however, how they will be supporting them: through discussion, writing, reading, questioning, etc.

There can be more than one differentiation approach happening within a lesson. Each part of a lesson should consider the way each child will be supported and should be identified on the plan in some way.

Summary of key points

An RE activity should match the RE learning objective, so when you are creating an activity and thinking about differentiation, consider whether the task you are providing will enhance and help achieve the objective or detract from it. Ask yourself *IS this activity developing PLTS in RE or is it a barrier to it?* Then consider how you will support the child's learning through a selection of differentiation techniques.

- Planning is like a Russian doll, as the short-term plans (STP) nest into the medium-term plans (MTP) and they in turn nest within the long-term plans (LTP). The objectives for each lesson can be found within the MTP, which in turn comes from the LTP
- There are different ways of creating a MTP. First create a topic or themed plan; then structure the ideas into an order and relate them to the objectives of the LTP
- Thematic and cross-curricular plans can be addressed in an MTP through either the objectives of two subjects being taught simultaneously or having two MTPs for two different subjects; and occasionally the links betweenn the two subjects and those between the two objectives in the two different plans become obvious
- STP has usually a beginning, middle and end but can sometimes have three or four activities incorporated into the middle
- Differentiation and assessment are crucial to planning
- When planning, try to remember to consider the mnemonic GOTOS for differentiation
- There can be more than one type of differentiation within a lesson
- Figures 10.1–10.5 are examples of themed plans, medium-term plans and short-term plans

Chapter 11
Creatively assessing Religious Education

LEARNING OBJECTIVES

In this chapter we will consider:

- The purpose of planning and assessment
- Various assessments in RE
- How to assess RE
- RE Level Descriptors

It will also address elements within the following Standards:

Q3a, Q3b, Q10, Q11, Q12, Q13, Q19, Q20, Q26a, Q26b, Q27

Introduction

This chapter will guide you towards an understanding of how to develop assessment techniques so that you have an awareness of how you can help your class achieve Attainment Targets 1 and 2 in Religious Education (QCA, 2004:34).

The planning cycle

As discussed in Chapter 10, planning and assessment are closely related. In fact, the planning process starts with reviewing what the children know and understand. Figure 11.1 shows how the process is cyclical and starts with assessment and ends with evaluation which inevitably leads into assessment again so that you are building on prior skills.

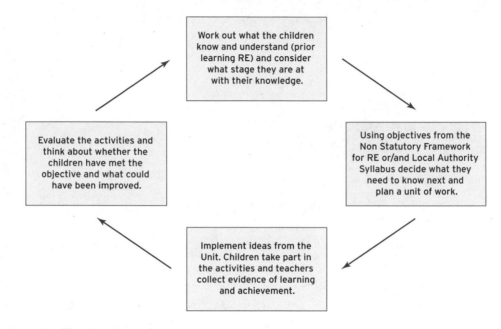

Figure 11.1 The planning cycle

This means that assessment is the start of the process and an essential element of the planning for learning and teaching. There is a vast amount of complex theory about assessment and it is quite a difficult concept; however, I will try to explain assessment as simply as possible so that you can begin to understand the various forms. Some useful texts for further reading into assessment would be Black and William (1998), Clarke (2005) and Briggs *et al.* (2008).

What is assessment in RE?

Assessment is the name given to the methods you use to find out what a child knows and understands (K&U) about an area of Religious Education such as what they K&U about religious stories, sacred spaces, pilgrimage, etc. Once you have discovered this, you can decide the skills that they need to further develop and then plan activities to help them achieve this (this is called Formative Assessment) or use what you found out as a way to sum up what they K&U at the end of a unit and give them a grade or level (this is called Summative Assessment).

'We forgive and the world is better'

'We forgive each other'

'This is God singing'

'I would give a hug from me'

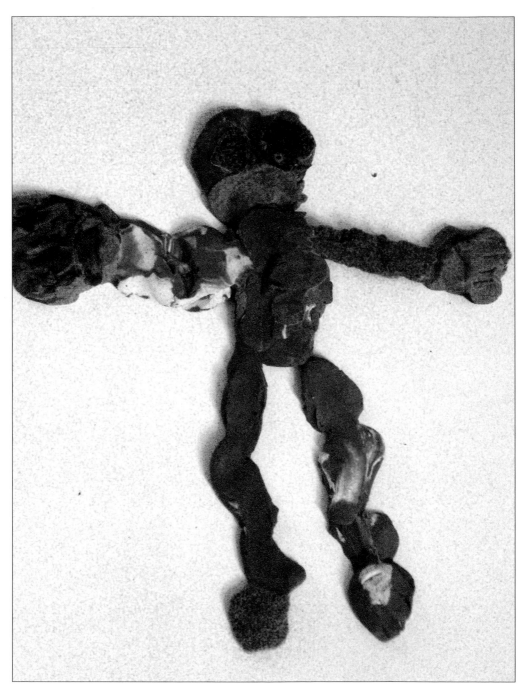

'I would give my soul'

'Jesus' love is red'

'We see birds every day'

'Each colour is happiness and love'

'I feel God's love'

'I feel squirly'

Illustration by Catherine Brogna

There are 2 attainment targets in RE that need to be assessed: Attainment Target 1 (AT1) is Learning *about* religion and Attainment Target 2 (AT2) is Learning *from* religion (see Chapter 1).

Assessing AT1 requires you to consider what the children **know** about religion; however, AT2 is more difficult to assess as it necessitates a child to reflect, interpret, respond imaginatively and discuss a variety of religious concepts and include personal opinion. Assessing these skills requires a more sensitive approach, because measuring emotions and opinions is complicated and it is always best to be objective when assessing. It is difficult for the assessment not to become subjective, because a strong religious faith may be interpreted by a non-specialist as an extreme religious view and therefore inappropriately judged, so it is best to be aware of what you should and shouldn't assess and be sensitive to children's privacy (McCreery *et al.*, 2008), e.g., don't assess religious commitment, but do assess particular views of religious concepts and how the child relates this to others.

How do I assess RE?

Briggs *et al.* (2008:2) suggest that there are three different types of assessment: assessment of learning; assessment for learning; and assessment as learning. The first is summative assessment, whereby a teacher assesses what a child knows and gives a grade, whereas the second is formative assessment, where the teacher discovers what a child knows and understands and then uses this to help plan how to develop skills in future lessons. Both of these are useful for assessment in RE as the former is appropriate for end of year reports and the latter is suitable for weekly planning schedules. However, for creative planning and the development of Personal Learning and Thinking Skills (PLTS) I feel that assessment *as* learning is more appropriate within an RE lesson, because it encourages metacognition and therefore requires the child to reflect on how they learn and what helps them learn so that they can be more in control of their own study (Jacques and Hyland, 2000:55, 56; see also Chapter 3).

Traditionally, assessment has always been seen as the teacher's role, but in today's educational climate, teaching assistants, learning mentors and children are taking a more active role. The way they do this is through discussion on what they have learnt, setting targets and undertaking self- or peer assessment.

Self- and peer assessment

Self-assessment is part of the personalised learning agenda and requires children to consider what they have learnt. The QCA (www.qca.org.uk) suggest that children will improve most when they understand the aim of the lesson and where they relate to it, thereby having ownership of the process. Clarke (2005) and Pollard (2005) both believe that children should be empowered to unlock their own knowledge and become reflective learners, hence the need to be aware of, and ideally understand, the assessment process.

To be able to do this, the children should take part in self-assessment within an RE lesson and need to be provided with a learning criterion so that they can use it to figure out how far along they are in meeting the skills and concepts identified. This can be done either through marking their written work using *I can* statements based on the Level Descriptors from the *Non Statutory Framework for Religious Education* (QCA, 2004:35-7) or through a more informal style of self-assessment, where they use a visual cue to help them reflect on their learning within a lesson such as a thumbs up, middle or down sign or including a smiley or sad face in their work book to show how much of the objective they feel they understand.

Peer assessment is similar, in that the children assess their work with a peer. This is not simply swapping work and giving feedback, but is a process where the children need to be trained into understanding the criteria that the work is based on so that they then have the ability to recognise features within it. It is quite a complex process that takes time to master. Through undertaking peer assessment and learning how to give reflective but critical feedback, the children will actively learn the skills needed to become competent learners within a subject. However, as Briggs *et al.* suggest, children need to be comfortable with self-assessment before being introduced to peer assessment (2008:31), so that they can understand that the process is more important than the outcome.

If you use these assessment methods as a learning tool within an RE lesson, make sure you remember the cyclical nature of the planning process, as there is no point in assessing if it doesn't in some way feed into future learning. The only exception is when you want to use it as a summative example of where they are within their learning at a given moment. This intention then needs to be explicit in your planning.

Teacher assessments

When assessing work it is usually good practice to indicate what the child has done well and provide guidance on how to improve. This can be done through providing written or verbal feedback that is called 'two stars and a wish', i.e. two things the child has done well and one way of improving. Teacher assessments can be immediate, through verbal praise and individual or collective feedback, or written after the lesson has finished. Either way, it is important that you always remember what it is that you want the children to know, understand and do and then reflect on whether they have achieved it in part or fully.

Frequently, in my experience, when a trainee teacher assesses a piece of written work they seem to mark the spelling, grammar and composition of the piece rather than the RE element of it. They are able to give feedback that is constructive, but not relevant to the learning objective of the lesson. It is crucial when assessing RE work that you and the children are very clear on what you want to see in the outcome. For example, if the objective is to reflect on a special (religious) journey and explain how they (or a religious person) felt at different locations (either pictorially, through a written piece or verbally through drama) then the assessment should be based on whether the children can explain or demonstrate emotions, can explore why the journey and locations are special and indicate whether they are able to relate it to a religious pilgrimage rather than whether it was a good piece of written work or a well performed drama.

What evidence shows learning in RE?

Using a selection of approaches to teach creative RE, you are likely to be provided with ample assessment opportunities. Creative RE lessons should provide you with a wealth of evidence that demonstrates a child's knowledge and understanding. Evidence of learning in RE can be shown through:

Art work (see Chapter 5)

Concept mapping

Dance (see Chapter 6)

Demonstrations of religious practice

Diagrams

Drama (see Chapter 7)

Drawings

Games

Labelling

Lyrics to a song (writing or reflecting)

Modelling – bringing in items from home

Musical composition (see Chapter 8)

Observing a child/group to see what they are discussing and doing

One-to-one discussion about an issue

Poetry

Photographs

Presentations

Questioning specific children

Quiz

Recounting

Stories

Tests

This is not an exhaustive list, there are many more examples of evidence that can help you assess a child's religious knowledge and understanding. But it is important to consider how the evidence, along with the Level Descriptors of the Non Statutory Framework, are used to help you make an assessment of a child's learning in AT1 and AT2.

Case Study — Assessing AT2 - Pictures as assessment

Whilst undertaking some Action Research about cross-curricular learning with Art and RE, I discovered that art was an effective way of identifying children's real thoughts and emotions. Many of the teachers I spoke to in the school found assessing AT2 difficult, because most tasks in the RC scheme of work seemed to be AT1 focused but when they did acquire evidence of AT2 they felt many of the responses from the children were text book answers - they wrote what they felt they *should* say and not necessarily what they truly felt.

Through using pastels, plasticine, paint and collage over a series of lessons, I observed that the children began to produce personal responses to big questions and formed opinions on what they felt about God and Easter.

One interesting assessment was of child B. His written responses were always exciting and contained lots of religious and emotional language. He was able to write and discuss what the

Roman Catholic response was to Easter and Lent and so his AT1 knowledge was very good, but when the class teacher and I tried to probe how he felt about Easter and Lent, his written responses seemed to lack personal reflection.

On one occasion, we asked B and his classmates to draw what they would give God during Lent. Because Roman Catholics believe God gave his only son to Christians, we wanted them to reflect on what they would give that was precious to them. B's written response was, '*I would give God my bear because it is special and God is special*' and his art response was a plasticine bear (Photograph 11.1). His written response seemed to suggest that he understood about giving something precious to God, but when I asked him about his art response and what would he give God, his verbal answer was,

'My second best toy.'

'Your *second* best toy? Why your *second* best one?'

'Well, I wouldn't give him my *first* would I?'

Photograph 11.1 B bear

This made me laugh, but with a view to assessment it showed a true sense of what B felt about God and his relationship with Him. It made me realise that B was not as advanced with AT2 as he was with AT1. His other art work for 'How did the disciples feel on the inside when blessed by the Holy Spirit at Pentecost?' (See Photograph 11.2) and 'How do you feel when you make good choices?' (See Photograph 11.3) showed that he was quite egocentric, as they depicted him in the centre and looked similar even though the lessons were 3 weeks apart, suggesting that he needed more opportunity to reflect visually and verbally on what he thinks and feels in order to relate religious experience to personal ideas and thoughts.

Photograph 11.2 BA

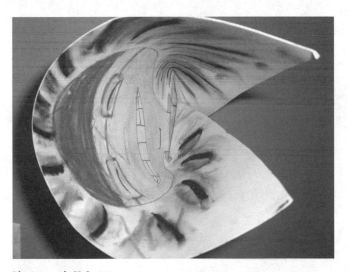

Photograph 11.3 BB

The opposite seemed to happen with other children in the class. Whereas the written work made it difficult for some children to express what they thought and in some cases became a barrier, the art allowed the children to be more reflective and experimental with their ideas. The work demonstrated a much more reflective attitude towards God, big questions and religious concepts. Photographs 11.4 to 11.10 are the children's responses to what would you give God for Lent (a glass pig, my guardian angel, a hug and my soul) and what does happiness and God's love look like? ('Jesus' love is red'; 'We see birds everyday and they carry God's love'; and 'each colour is happiness and love mixed together'; see also colour plate section').

Each image and verbal response hint towards how children are viewing the world they live in and how they feel about life, love, God, etc. Hence, Art to me seems to be a fantastic method for assessing AT2 through personal reflections and opinions about religion.

Photograph 11.4 'I Would give my pig'

Photograph 11.5 'I would give my guardian angel'

Photograph 11.6 'I would give a hug from me'

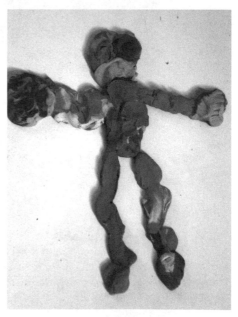

Photograph 11.7 'I would give my soul'

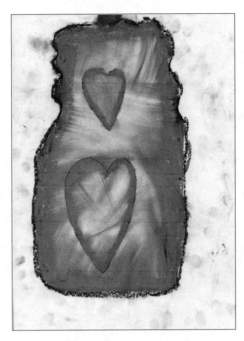

Photograph 11.8 'Jesus' love is red'

Photograph 11.9 'We see birds every day'

Photograph 11.10 'Each colour is happiness and love'

Source: Year 3 in a Roman Catholic (RC) Primary School Preston, Lancashire

How do I collect evidence?

Assessment is something that can create mountains of paperwork, because some teachers seem to worry about having the right sort of evidence for Ofsted, the Local Authority RE advisor, governors, the Diocese and parents to prove that they are teaching RE effectively. Thus it can become onerous and a paper exercise with no real focus. Assessing in RE should be thought about in advance and have a clear aim so it can become a useful tool for learning and teaching (Kyriacou, 1998: 120, 121).

The outcome from planned activities, e.g., the Art, Dance, Drama and Music, will become your evidence of the children's learning and achievement. So, when planning for RE and considering assessment at the same time, think about what you need (and don't need) to collect so that you are clear on what evidence will be produced and can make purposeful assessments. Ask yourself the following five questions:

Why am I assessing?

Be clear on whether you are assessing for a grade (assessment *of* learning), for a learning tool (assessment *as* learning) or to inform future learning (assessment *for* learning). This will then help you focus on what you are assessing and help you create activities that provide you with the evidence you need to assess appropriately.

Its also a good idea to reflect on what you will do with the assessment, for example: keep it as a running record of a child's progression; as a celebratory display on parents evening; or for target setting in the children's targets book, otherwise you are assessing and collecting evidence for no real purpose, making it pointless.

What am I assessing?

Focus on the RE learning objective and always remember what it is that you want the children to have achieved by the end of the lesson. Be clear on what it is you want to assess (e.g. a child's use of religious vocabulary) and what you want to do with the assessment (e.g. to inform planning or target setting, etc.).

When do I assess?

Consider when you intend to do the assessment. Consider if you will assess at the end of the lesson or during it, as this will have an impact on the type of assessment you do and who you will assess.

How do I assess?

Consider how you want to collect any data. Will it be a written piece at the end of the lesson? Will you take photos of a drama? Will it be a podcast on the school website?

Whom am I assessing?

You don't have to assess every child in every RE lesson, in fact it is impossible to do so (Pollard, 1997:283). It is best to focus on a group and ensure that, over time, you have assessed everyone. Who you assess depends on the type of assessment you are undertaking. If you want to assess through a written piece and are marking after the lesson then you are assessing everyone. However, it is more difficult to assess everyone when the method of collection is observation or dance.

Levelling a child in RE

The RE Level Descriptors are linked to the two Attainment Targets and are statements that provide an overview of what a child should be achieving at a certain point in their learning (QCA, 2004:35-7). They start at Level 1 and finish at Level 8 with exceptional performance and are based on the National Curriculum's concept of the spiral curriculum, whereby children revisit skills and objectives throughout their education, but each time at a more difficult stage. At the end of KS1 a child is expected to have achieved or be generally working within the Level 2 category of both attainment targets, whereas at the end of KS2 they should have achieved or be within the Level 4 category.

When assessing evidence such as an account of a trip to a place of worship or art work created in an RE lesson, it is a good idea to review the descriptor and see which is the level that 'best fits' what is being shown in the work. One piece of evidence, however, may not be a good example for assessing a child's full capabilities, but over a period of time the child will have produced a selection of evidence, which when put together will provide you with a better overview of what they know and understand in RE, allowing you to give a summative assessment. Sometimes it is a good idea to translate some of the Level Descriptors into 'I can' statements, such as 'I can begin to see similarities in religions' (based on Level 1 AT1), as this may help you work out the various factors that make up a full level and then be able to measure what a child has done and what they haven't. This would also make it easier for the children to use within peer or self-assessment.

When wishing to use the level descriptors as a mode for Formative Assessment it is a good idea to look at the level above the one the child is working at and use it as a target for improvement, i.e. if they are working at Level 2 then use some areas of Level 3 as a target. Yet if they haven't achieved all of the level and are working within it then make the target something that is listed in the level descriptor and which they haven't yet achieved.

Case Study

Year 3 sample – assessing forgiveness using the Level Descriptors

The objective was from the Roman Catholic (RC) *The Way, the Truth and the Life* scheme of work – to consider how people forgive and know what Jesus taught about forgiveness.

The children were asked to look at a painting of the Prodigal Son and, after retelling the story, discuss the messages within it. They related it to Jesus' teachings of forgiveness and love. They had four questions to respond to:

1. Do you like the painting?
2. Why do you/don't you like it?
3. What is your favourite part of the painting?
4. Draw what you think would be a symbol of love.

K's response shows

The second and third answers of K's work show that he understands the message in the story. However, answer 3 and the image show that K has an awareness of how the story related to the RC view of the Holy Spirit loving someone.

This shows that K is working in Level 2 of AT1. He is able to retell stories and suggest meanings for actions and symbols. He can identify how religion is expressed in different ways. His other work (not shown here) also demonstrates that he is confident at Level 2 and so should have a target that comes from Level 3 AT1, possibly recognising similarities and differences in the key features of religions.

J's response

J's answers demonstrate that he is able to understand the messages from the Prodigal Son story and relate it to the painting. He links the third answer to the symbol he drew and his verbal response was, 'This is my dad hugging me when I'm sorry for being bad.'

K

1 yes I do

2 because it's a good sine of love because there is the father Love tho the son.
3 the father and the son
the father is forgiving the son, because he said that he shuddnt be his son.

4

It is the Holy spirit coming down, Loving some won.

J

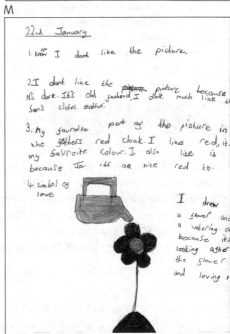

22nd January

1. Yes I do like the picture

2.I like the picture because It Shows for givness and how much the mon loves his Son

3. my favouriede part of the picture is them hugging because it show that whatever you do his dad wont stop loving you

M

22nd January

1. No I dont like the picture.

2.I dont like the picture it's dark. It's old fashend. I don't much like the Son's clotes aather.

3. My favorite part of the picture in the fathers red cloak. I like red, it's my savroite colour. I also like it because its an nice red to.

4. simbol of love

I drew a flower and a watering ca because its looking after the flower and loving i

This shows that J is also working at Level 2 of AT1, as the work has similar features to K's. However, J's work also shows some evidence of AT2 level 2. The symbol that J created is very personal and his verbal response shows that he is showing that he can 'respond sensitively to … their own and other's experiences [and] … in matters of right and wrong they recognise their own values' (QCA, 2004:36).

M's response

M's answers are limited. They do not show much evidence of religious understanding and she is focusing on the art rather than making a link between the religious story and the painting. This could be because the questions are too open and she is unsure of what is expected of her, it could also mean she does not know what the learning criterion is, i.e., the learning objective. However, the broadness of the questions does allow an assessment of her religious awareness, as her answers were honest.

The final question shows some understanding of love and how, according to M, love means nurture. This touches on AT1 Level 2, because she suggests symbols for actions. It could possibly also link to AT2 Level 2, because she is able to respond to her experiences. M needs more opportunity to demonstrate her AT1 knowledge, so this needs to be planned within the next few RE lessons.

The outcome of this work was varied, showing that a snapshot of a lesson can only show part of an assessment, possibly because the task maybe too broad and doesn't offer much of an opportunity to show elements of religious knowledge or it could be that it only allows part of the knowledge to be shown. Thus, it is a good idea to collect a selection of samples so that you can have a broader view of the capabilities of the child, making the overall assessment more accurate.

To develop your knowledge further it might be useful to look on the QCA website National Curriculum in Action (http://curriculum.qca.org.uk/key-stages-1-and-2/index.aspx), where there is a selection of examples of KS1 and 2 assessments of RE that link a piece of work to a Level Descriptor and so should be beneficial to you in helping you become aware of how to annotate and assess a piece of written work in RE.

Summary of key points

Assessment is a complex issue. It takes time and experience to become familiar with the various facets of it, so don't worry if you are confused. It is advisable to become as familiar as possible with the content of the Level Descriptors and Programmes of Study of the Non Statutory Framework for RE (QCA, 2004) so that you are aware of what a child should be trying to achieve at a certain Key Stage.

On the whole, the key points of this chapter have been:

- Assessment is part of the planning cycle so, when planning, think about and plan for assessment
- Assessment is finding out what a child knows and understands in RE
- According to Briggs *et al.* (2008:2) there are three types of assessment:

  1. Assessment of learning
  2. Assessment for learning
  3. Assessment as learning

- Assessment can be conducted by the children as learners, by their peers or you as the teacher

- Remember to always assess the objectives of RE and not be confused into assessing the way it is presented. Assessment must relate to the RE learning objective of the lesson
- Use two stars and a wish as verbal or written feedback
- There are many ways of presenting learning in RE that can form evidence that you can keep and assess
- When planning, begin to consider assessment and think about the evidence you want to collect. Asking the following five questions should help you stay focused:

  1. Why am I assessing?
  2. What am I assessing?
  3. When do I assess?
  4. How do I assess?
  5. Whom am I assessing?

- RE Level Descriptors are linked to the Attainment Targets. It is good to translate them into 'I can' statements
- Use the Level Descriptors as a way to assess what a child knows and understands now and what they need to know and understand in the future. This can then become a target that informs future planning and/or target setting for the children

Chapter 12
What do I need to know?

LEARNING OBJECTIVES

In this chapter we will consider:

- Basic knowledge that will help future study into the six major faith traditions in the UK
- Themes that are within all six major faith traditions
- The lack of confidence you may have in regards to subject knowledge
- Where you can gain further information to help you develop your RE subject knowledge

It will also address elements within the following Standards:

Q3, Q7, Q14, Q15

I don't know about religion, so I don't teach it!

It has been suggested through many studies (e.g. L'Anson, 2004; McCreery, 2005; Revell, 2005) that trainee teachers and, in fact, many new teachers worry about their lack of knowledge of the six major faith traditions and, because of this, lack the confidence to teach it. The studies identified that trainee teachers seemed not to realise that they had an awareness of teaching methods already used within Literacy or History lessons, such as hot seating or analysis of text, which could be transferred to RE to help stimulate personal reflection and development of Key Skills (William, 2005:46). They seemed too hung up on their lack of knowledge to realise this, making them uncreative in their RE teaching.

Unfortunately, the trainees and class teachers tended to see RE as more about transferring knowledge of the nuts and bolts of a religion, i.e. what, where, when and why as explored in Attainment Target 1 (McCreery, 2005:273-4), rather than as an opportunity to help children gain a sense of identity and encourage personal growth. As we have explored in Chapter 1, Religious Education has two Attainment Targets, AT2 is concerned with personal reflection, opinion and consideration about puzzling life questions, whereas AT1 is about gaining knowledge about religions. Both Attainment Targets need to be taught so that there is a balance of learning opportunity. Together they provide opportunities for children to consider what they know and understand about how and why people live in the way they choose. If only one of the Attainment Targets were taught, a child's holistic learning would be negatively affected, thus the purpose of this chapter is to help you begin to address some of the basic knowledge that you require to help you implement the creative approaches suggested and discussed throughout this book.

How can I develop my confidence in subject knowledge?

It is impossible for you to know everything about every religion, so having a little basic information is important, as it can be used as a stepping stone to help you gain confidence. If you have little or no subject knowledge (which seems quite common with many of the trainees I teach) it is useful to have a starting point such as key vocabulary or a piece of basic information to help you know where to begin your research. This chapter will start you off with a brief overview of some of the themes addressed in the Non Statutory Framework and which are likely to be in many different syllabi. It will also suggest some texts and websites to help you take your study further.

Common themes in Local Authority syllabi and references to the *Non Statutory Framework for Religious Education* (2004)

	Key Stage 1	Key Stage 2
Places of worship: Sacred spaces	2a, 3c, 3l, 3m	1d, 2a, 3c, 3g, 3n
Religious texts/story	1a, 3f	1a, 1b, 1f, 3f, 3g, 3i
Religious leaders	1c, 3i	3j
Celebrations and festivals	1b, 3g, 3f	1e, 2b, 3l
Rites of passage	2a	2b, 3g, 3l, 3p
Rules and regulations	1a, 1b	1b, 1e, 3g, 3h

The content of Local Authority syllabi should be based on the *Non Statutory Framework for Religious Education* (QCA, 2004) and cover the areas of puzzling questions, enquiry, reflection and discussion into the six major faith traditions. Often, the learning is organised into themes such as within *Living Difference: The Agreed Syllabus for Hampshire, Portsmouth and Southampton* (July 2004); *The Lancashire Agreed Syllabus for Religious Education* (2001) and *The East Riding of Yorkshire Agreed Syllabus for Religious Education* (2005). These syllabi contain themes that are similar to the table above and focus on Key Skills. Occasionally, however, the learning in syllabi may be organised into distinct religions with a focus on fundamental principles or life questions, which broadly explore some comparative areas such as text, story, symbols, places of worship and celebration, e.g. *The Devon Plymouth and Torbay Agreed Syllabus for RE* (2001); *Shropshire Agreed Syllabus for RE* (2004) and the *Wirral Agreed Syllabus for Religious Education* (2007). You will usually find most syllabi on the Local Authority website or you could do a Google search, where you will find a host of sites that will take you directly to various syllabi across the UK. It's a good idea to find the Agreed Syllabus for the Local Authority that you work in and keep it as a PDF or word file on your memory stick, so that you can quickly refer to it when you are planning your RE lessons.

Whichever way you decide to teach RE (through separate religions and theology or through common themes), you need enough knowledge to feel confident teaching it. The following tables are designed to give you a small glimpse into the general points that will help you answer basic questions. The content of the tables is limited and is here for you to use as a springboard into further study. In other words, it's a place to start!

Sacred spaces – Places of worship

	Buddhism	Christianity	Hinduism	Islam	Judaism	Sikhism
Name	Temple and home	**Church**	Mainly home with a **ghar mandir** (shrine) also at times go to temple (**mandir**)	**Mosque**	**Synagogue**	**Gurdwara** (doorway of the **guru**)
Day of devotion	**Puja** (devotion) happens in the morning and evening. On half or full moon	Sunday yet some services are on a Saturday	3 times a day. Morning, noon and night at home. Don't have to attend temple but in UK attendance is usually on a Sunday	Friday	Friday/Saturday Jewish men say prayers at home	Usually Sunday in the UK
Special dress?	No special dress	No special dress	No special dress	Dress modestly with loose clothing; shoes removed before entering	Men wear a **kippa/yarmulke** to cover the top of their head	Dress modestly with loose clothing; shoes removed before entering
What happens?	Lighting of incense, display of prayer flags and wheels. Devotion with blessings to a shrine of **Buddha**	Sharing of bread and wine to remember last meal with Jesus called the **Eucharist** **Protestant Christians** believe it is an act of remembrance whereas **Roman Catholic Christians** believe it to be a Sacrament (God is present in the bread and wine)	**Puja** (worship) usually involves lighting a lamp called **arti** and lighting incense, ghee or oil Worship is to a Hindu deity or many deities presented as **murtis** (sacred images or icons of **deities**). It involves blessings with the fire	Communal prayer facing **Mecca** (holiest place in Islam). **Mihrab** is part of the mosque that shows the direction of Mecca An area is designated for **wudu** (ritual washing) which prepares Muslims for prayer	In orthodox synagogues men and women sit separately Prayers are said by a **rabbi** from the **Torah,** which is read aloud from a raised part of the synagogue called a **bimah**	Men and women read from the **Guru Granth Sahib** and music is played with drums and sitars The community then sit together and have a communal meal (**langar**) cooked by one of the families on a rotation basis

	Buddhism	Christianity	Hinduism	Islam	Judaism	Sikhism
Name	Dhamma/Dharma	Bible – Old and New Testaments	Upanishads The Mahabharata The Ramayana	Qur'an/Koran	Torah Tenakh	Guru Granth Sahib
What does it contain?	A selection of sayings, and guidance written by **Siddhartha Gautama** who became known as **Buddha**	**Old Testament** A selection of books and poetry that help to guide the early Jewish people and Christians **New Testament** A selection of books called **Gospels** from disciples and letters from early Christians such as **Saint Paul**	Most are written in Sanskrit and called **vedas** (knowledge). Divided in **Smirti** and **Shruti** They contain allegorical stories and are often wrapped in silk or cotton and treated with great respect. They are based on the oral tradition	Written in Arabic and considered to be the word of **Allah** (God) It contains teachings about life, God and stories about the Prophet **Muhammad** The Qur'an is considered to be the ultimate source of guidance	**Tenakh** is the Hebrew Bible and contains the Law, Psalms, Prophets and writings. It contains five books from the Old Testament (**Torah**) with the laws that Jews follow in their daily life Interpretations of teachings is in the **Talmud** written by Jewish **rabbis**	Contains **hymns** that give guidance to Sikhs that are part of the daily prayer It has a special room in people's homes. It is believed that God is revealed through the text as he was through the ten **Gurus** that came before it
How do people use the religious texts?	Buddhist monks (who wear orange) learn parts by heart and recite them on special occasions	**Scripture** is read during services and then discussed by the priest in a **sermon** or **liturgy**	Prayers are often recited before reading from the texts **Mantras** are within the texts and are recited	**Muslims** read the Qur'an every day and it is an important part of worship and daily life Children learn to read it in after school classes	There is a Hebrew handwritten copy of the Torah (**Sefer Torah**) held in the synagogue in a specially designed cupboard called an **Ark** (**Aron Ha-Kodesh**)	The **Guru Granth Sahib** is respected and read, but not revered like the Torah or the Qur'an, and is handled with great respect. When is moved it has to be covered and accompanied with five men (**khalsa**)

	Buddhism	Christianity	Hinduism	Islam	Judaism	Sikhism
Name	**Buddha** means 'The Awakened' or 'Enlightened'	**The Trinity**	Many deities, although Hindus talk of a **Trinity**	**Allah** **The Prophet** **Muhammad**	**Jehovah/Yahweh** **Abraham** **Moses**	**God** (Nam Japna; Satnam) **Guru Nanak**
Why they are important	**Siddhartha Gautama** (Buddha) was a human who made it his responsibility to teach people how to live in perfect wisdom and compassion. He realised that people are usually greedy and so they needed help to be at peace and practise **The Four Noble Truths and Eightfold Path**	Christianity is monotheistic yet God is made up of 3 ways of Being (like a clover leaf) **God the Father** - God is the Giver of life (Creator) **God the Son** - God became human in Jesus Christ to help mankind (Sustainer) **God the Holy Spirit** - God is everywhere (Redeemer) **Jesus** is the core of Christianity and is also called **Lord** (teacher) or **Christ** (the annointed one)	Trinity - **Brahma** the Creator, **Vishnu** the Sustainer and **Shiva** the Destroyer God is manifested in many ways through male and female deities called **avatars** Popular gods are **Lakshmi, Rama, Krishna, Ganesha** and **Kali**	**Muhammad** was the final Prophet. Muslims usually say 'Peace be upon him' after his name Muslims believe the **Angel Gabriel** appeared to him near **Mecca** and told him to memorise text (the **Qur'an**) and bring people to worship one true God (**Allah**). Allah has 100 names, although only the camel knows the 100th! Muhammad is seen as God's messenger to the Islamic world	**God (Jehovah)** made a covenant with the Jewish community through Abraham and then Moses This **covenant** became a binding relationship. The Jewish people were considered chosen by God, and Abraham was their guide. When he died his leadership went to his son **Isaac** who then passed it onto his son, **Jacob** **Moses** was given the law by God on **Mount Sinai** and took the Jewish people out of slavery in Egypt	Sikhism is **monotheistic** yet God has many names. **Guru** in the Sikh faith means leading to truth Guru Nanak was the first Guru. He taught that everyone is equal. He preached about how to be a good person and established the first Sikh community The gurus are not worshipped, but are simply guides and role models

Religious leaders cont.

	Buddhism	Christianity	Hinduism	Islam	Judaism	Sikhism
Spiritual leader	The **Dalai Lama** of Tibet is believed to be reincarnations of former leaders	**The Pope** – head of the Roman Catholic Church **The Queen** – head of the Monarchy and head of the Church of England	Priests from the Brahmin **caste** The caste system sorts out the positions that people have in life, e.g., their jobs or family situation. Some Hindus feel a good caste is very important	The word of Allah (**Qur'an**) is what leads the community **Imams** help give religious direction and guide the community to be good Muslims	**Rabbis** are the leaders in the synagogues and conduct rites of passage and worship	**Guru Nanak** **Guru Angad Dev** **Guru Amar Dev** **Guru Arjan Dev** **Guru Hargobid** **Guru Har Rai** **Guru Har Krishnan** **Guru Tegh Bahadur Guru** **Gobind Singh**
People who help within the religion	Monk Nun	**Archbishop** **Bishop** **Canon** **Priest** **Nun** **Monk** Different **denominations** call a priest by various names such as **Preacher, Minister, Vicar**	**Priests** (priestly class) **Ksatryas** (soldiers) **Vaishvas** (farmers) **Shudras** (manual labourers) **Harijans** (the untouchables) The **caste** system is hierarchical	**Imam** (means leader or model)	Mothers are considered as having a very important role in Judaism as they are at the centre of religious practice and many of the festivals	Spiritual leaders

Celebrations and festivals

	Buddhism	Christianity	Hinduism	Islam	Judaism	Sikhism
Details of the religious festivals These are some of the celebrations yet there are more festivals and celebrations within each faith tradition	**Wesak** or **Buddha day** – May. This festival celebrates the life and teaching of Buddha. People decorate homes and temples with flowers	**Advent** and **Christmas** – December. Christians count the days to Christmas. They light weekly candles in church services on a Sunday. **Christmas** celebrates the birth of Jesus. People give gifts and decorate their house with lights and colour	**Holi** – March/April. Festival of colours. Traditionally liquid dyes and coloured powder are thrown at each other. There are also bonfires. It is associated with stories of **Vishnu** and his devotees	**Eid ul-Fitr** – (Big Eid). There is a month of fasting called **Ramadan** as a run up to this festival. Muslims fast from sun up to sun down and pray at the Mosque every day. The fasting is broken with the festival. Muslims send gifts to each other, buy new clothes and have special family meals	**Shabbat** – candles are lit and family have a Sabbath meal on the Friday. No work is done, no business happens or money carried. It's a day of rest. It is to remember God resting on the seventh day, which is written in the Torah	**Gurpurb** – various festivals that remember the lives of different gurus such as **Guru Nanak's** birthday in November and lasts for 3 days and **Guru Gobind Singh's** birthday in January
	Dhammacakka – around July. Anniversary of Buddha's first sermon. People visit monks and take them gifts then hear them preach and read from the scripture	**Shrove Tuesday** – the day before Lent. Popular custom is to make pancakes **Ash Wednesday** is the first day of Lent. Ashes are put on the forehead of Christians as a symbol of **penitence**	**Rama Navami** – March/April. Hindus celebrate Rama's birthday. An icon of Rama is put in a crib in the temple	**Eid ul-Adha** – (Little Eid). This is a festival that remembers Abraham's obedience to God when He asked him to kill his son. A lamb was sacrificed instead and so sacrificing a lamb is part of the festival	**Hanukkah** – December. It's sometimes called the Festival of Lights. It is to commemorate the conquest of the Maccabees in 168 BCE. It marks the miracle of religious oil lasting for 8 days and not 1	**Installations of the Guru Granth Sahib** This happens in August-September

Celebrations and festivals cont.

Buddhism	Christianity	Hinduism	Islam	Judaism	Sikhism
	Lent and **Easter** – Spring (dates change with moon phases). Lent is a time when Christians prepare for Easter and reflect on how God is with them in adversity. **Easter** celebrates Jesus' death and **resurrection**. It's the most important festival	**Jammashtami** – August/September. Celebrates Krishna's birth. Icon of Krishna is pushed in a swing by members of the community and they perform **pujas**		**Pesach/Passover** – March/April. Story of the escape from Egypt. Symbolic food put on a **Seder plate** to remember the **Israelites**	**Vaisakhi** – this usually happens on 13 April and celebrates the days of 1699 when Guru Gobind Singh founded the **Khalsa**. Sikhs replace flag (**Nishan Sahib**) that's on the Gurdwara
		Navaratri – 9 nights September/October. 10 days of celebration and is in honour of the goddess **Lakshmi**		**Purim** – Feb/March. A celebration of being a faithful Jew from the book of Ruth in the Old Testament. Children take part in lots of role-play and drama	**Diwali** – October. This is usually to commemorate Guru Hargobind's return from imprisonment. A festival of deliverance and the **gurdwaras** are illuminated
		Diwali – October. Symbolises good over evil represented by **Rama and Sita.** Fireworks and **diva lamps** are lit			

	Buddhism	Christianity	Hinduism	Islam	Judaism	Sikhism
A rite of passage is when a person moves from one state of their life into another, e.g., from single life to married life. This occasion is usually marked with a religious ceremony **There are secular rites of passage such as degree ceremonies** **Most religious rites of passage are to do with birth, marriage and death**	**Marriage** is not considered sacred, but when Buddhists do marry they exchange vows and occasionally a nun or monk will attend **Death** – bodies are cremated and the relatives help the dying person die peacefully so that their body is **reincarnated** with good **Karma**	**Baptism** or **Christening** – this is when an adult or child has holy water placed on their head or the adult is submerged in water as a ritual cleansing of evil **Confirmation** – a ceremony that teenagers tend to undertake and is an acceptance of their being an adult in the faith **Marriage** – happens in a church where the bride and groom exchange **vows.** Passages are read aloud from the Bible **Death** – Christians believe there is life after death and they enter Heaven with God. The body can be cremated or buried usually with a service where the priest reads passages from the Old and New Testaments	Undertake ceremonies about birth and death as they believe in **Reincarnation.** Hindus believe that the soul is reincarnated many times and is linked to **Karma** **Birth** – when a baby is in the womb the mother would read scriptures to the baby. When the baby's born and if he is a boy, he can sometimes take part in the **sacred thread ceremony,** whereby he is given 3 strands of thread to wear all the time **Marriage** – a long event where the bride and groom do different things. Occasionally marriages are arranged but only on the consent of both the boy and girl	**Birth** – the call to prayer is whispered in a newborn baby's ear. If a boy the baby will then soon be **circumcised** **Marriage** – Occasionally marriages are arranged but only on the consent of both the boy and girl. The woman wears red **Death** – once a person has died, the body is ritually washed and wrapped in a white cloth. The community say prayers	**Birth** – 8-day-old boys are **circumcised** by a trained Mohel. Girls are blessed **Bar Mitzvah** – a special ceremony for a 13-year-old boy who is now considered to be an adult and responsible for himself and to follow the Law. When a girl is 12 she undertakes a ceremony called **Bat Mitzvah** **Marriage** – a Jewish wedding takes place under a decorated canopy called a **Hupa** **Death** – the body is buried as soon as possible and annointed and wrapped in a white cloth. Mourning continues for 11 months	**Birth – mool mantra** (a hymn from the **Guru Granth Sahib**) is whispered into a new born baby's ear **Marriage** – the bride and groom walk around the **Guru Granth Sahib** during their ceremony. They wear red and garlands of flowers, etc. **Death** – the **Guru Granth Sahib** is read when someone dies and hymns are sung by the community

Rites of passage cont.

Buddhism	Christianity	Hinduism	Islam	Judaism	Sikhism
	The Roman Catholic Church include other rites of passage (**Sacraments**): **First Confession** – where a child will ask for forgiveness from God through a Priest **First Holy Communion** – a child will take the Eucharist for the first time	**Death** – the body is cremated as soon as possible to help reincarnation			

Rules and regulations

	Buddhism	Christianity	Hinduism	Islam	Judaism	Sikhism
Name	**The Four Noble Truths** **The Eightfold Path**	**10 Commandments** (Old Testament) **1 Commandment** (New Testament)	Openness to the divine – this happens through a variety of practices	**Five Pillars of Islam**	**The Shema**	**Five Ks** – called this because they all begin with K
What are they?	**Four Noble Truths** 1 – all existence is suffering 2 – the cause of suffering is desire 3 – getting rid of desire puts an end to suffering and leads to enlightenment 4 – the path to enlightenment is open to all people (through the **Eightfold Path**) These are the major teachings that Buddha taught in his first sermon Meditation is important in Buddhism	Worship no other God Don't worship other images Don't use God's name in vain Observe the Sabbath Respect your parents Don't commit murder Don't commit adultery Don't steal Don't lie Don't be envious Given to Moses by God who was revealed to him through a bush that was alight with a sacred flame but did not become burnt (Exodus 20:2-17)	**Yoga** and **Dharma** – doing one's duty and choosing right action **Bhakti** – devotion to a deity Learning about the relationship between the soul and Brahma	1. **Shahadah** – declaration of faith *There is no God but Allah and Muhammad is his Prophet* 2. **Salat** – prayer which happens 5 times a day with specific rituals such as washing (**wudu**) 3. **Sawm** – fasting in the 9th month (**Ramadan**), between sun up and sun down 4. **Zakat** – annual % of wealth is given to help the poor 5. **Hajj** – pilgrimage to Mecca at least once in a lifetime	The **Shema** (Deuteronomy 6:4-7) *Hear O Israel: the Lord our God is one Lord, and you shall love the Lord your God with all your heart, and with all your soul and with all your might* This is the fundamental law of Judaism and a scroll of this passage is placed inside a small box called a **mezuzah** and put on the right hand door post of every Jewish house and in small boxes called **Tefillin** when Jewish men pray	**Kanga** – comb symbolises spiritual discipline **Kara** – steel bangle symbolises strength and goodness **Kachhahera** – breeches symbolises readiness **Kirpan** – sword symbolises readiness to fight for justice **Kesh** – long hair symbolises wisdom Each of these identify the brotherhood of Sikhs called **Khalsa**

Rules and regulations cont.

Buddhism	Christianity	Hinduism	Islam	Judaism	Sikhism
Eightfold Path 1 Right Knowledge 2 Right Thought 3 Right Speech 4 Right Actions 5 Right Livelihood 6 Right Effort 7 Right Mindfulness 8 Right Concentration Buddhists believe that Karma affects everyone. Everything has a consequence that will happen in this or a different life. This path helps Buddhists achieve good Karma	Matt 22:39 *Love your neighbour as you love yourself* This is sometimes called the **Great Commandment.** Jesus was asked by a Pharisee to say which is the greatest commandment of the Law. Jesus extended the Jewish law of the **Shema** and added another. This **Great Commandment** is considered to overrule any previous law		There are rules within Islam relating to food, i.e. what can and cannot be eaten, and how meat should be prepared (halal)	There are rules within Judaism for food preparation called **Kashrut** Milk and meat can't be cooked or eaten together and pork and most seafood such as prawns are not permitted to be eaten	

Where can I find further information?

It would be useful for you to re-read the case study within Chapter 9, 'Using creative resources' called 'What is the artefact and how would you use it to develop your own knowledge?' (see p. 87). Then undertake an audit of your own subject knowledge so that you are aware of what you need to study further. A blank template of a personal training plan is provided (adapted from Copley and Priestly, 1991:140) (see Figure 9.1, p. 89). This will help you consider what you already know and what you need to find out. It is advisable to audit what you know in themes or chunks of information, otherwise it can seem too daunting. Once you have conducted your audit, create a research question so that you are focused with what you need to find out, then use any of the following sources to help you.

Themes

There are many children's books that will be useful for you to read to acquire some information about a religion. Some are part of a series, so can be quite helpful in enabling you to make comparisons between the faith traditions. Although some of these texts are fairly old (1980s), they can still be useful in helping you to improve your knowledge about religion.

General information

Bowker, J. (2005) *The Concise Oxford Dictionary of World Religions*, Oxford, Oxford University Press

Breilly, E., O'Brien, P. and Martin, P. (2000) *Religions of the World: The Illustrated Guide to Origins, Beliefs, Traditions and Festivals*, London, Wayland Publishers

Cole Owen, C. (1996) *Six World Faiths*, London, Continuum

Fry, E. and Weller P. (1997) *Religions in the UK: A Multi-faith Directory*, Derby, University of Derby

Hinnells, J. (2003) *The New Penguin Handbook of Living Religions* (2nd edition), London, Penguin Publications

Langley, M. (1997) *Eyewitness Guide to Religion*, London, Dorling Kindersley

Lauhert, M. (ed.) (1999) *Religions of the World: A Collins Fact Book*, London, HarperCollins Publishers

McCreery, E., Palmer S. and Voiels, V. (2008) *Achieving QTS teaching Religious Education Primary and Early Years*, Exeter, Learning Matters

Wood, C. (2008) *100 Ideas for Teaching Religious Education*, London, Continuum

British Journal for Religious Education (BJRE)

REtoday magazine

REsource magazine

http://www.teachers.tv

Places of worship

http://pow.reonline.org.uk/
http://www.bbc.co.uk/religion/galleries/worship/

Religious texts

http://www.bl.uk/onlinegallery/sacredtexts/

Celebrations and festivals

Rose, D. and Rose, G. (1997) *A World of Faith Series: Passover*, London, Evans Brothers (lots of different celebrations and information about world religions)

http://www.bbc.co.uk/schools/religion/

http://www.shapworkingparty.org.uk/

http://www.hindukids.org/

Religious leaders

Bailey, J. (1987) *Religious Leaders and Places of Pilgrimage Today*, Huddersfield, Schofield & Sims

Rites of passage

http://www.bbc.co.uk/dna/h2g2/A521524

Mayled, J. (1986) *Religious Topics Series Death Customs*, London, Wayland Publishers

Mayled, J. (1986) *Religious Topics Series Marriage Customs*, London, Wayland Publishers

Mayled, J. (1986) *Religious Topics Series Birth Customs*, London, Wayland Publishers

Mayled, J. (1986) *Religious Topics Series Pilgrimage*, London, Wayland Publishers

Mayled, J. (1986) *Religious Topics Series Fasting and Feasting*, London, Wayland Publishers

(lots of different celebrations and information about world religions)

Rules and regulations

Senker, C. (2005) *Talking About my Faith Series*, London, Franklin Watts

(lots of different celebrations and information about world religions)

Chapter 13
'Of making many books there is no end'

(Ecclesiastes 12:12)

Because Initial Teacher Training providers have limited time in their Definitive Course Documents to provide many opportunities for trainee teachers to have an indepth understanding of the role and value of RE, it is essential to have useful texts that help. This book has tried to help you lose some of the worry that you may have about how to teach creative RE, what to teach in RE, how to plan for RE, how to use resources and where to get the information you don't have so that you develop your subject knowledge.

In Chapter 3 we explored how Religious Education should be about Key Skills. In particular the Personal Learning and Thinking Skills of:

- Communication
- Reflection
- Thinking
- Enquiry

Creative RE should try to ensure that these important skills are practised and developed, not only because they are essential to children becoming religiously literate, but also because they are essential life skills (QCA, 2004:9).

RE works well with other subjects within the foundation subjects so, whenever possible, try to connect them. However, always try to remember the subtle distinction between cross-curricular and thematic learning. Chapter 4 developed this is in detail but to remind you:

- Cross-curricular teaching is planning for and teaching specific learning objectives for at least two subjects simultaneously.
- Thematic teaching is teaching RE within a theme that links to other subjects.

Chapters 5, 6, 7 and 8 have provided you with advice and guidance on how to creatively connect RE with Art, Dance, Drama and Music. The case studies illustrate the suggested ideas within the chapters and are based on real examples from schools. The examples have been collected over the 14 years I have worked in education and are either from interviews with teachers, lessons I have observed or lessons and ideas I have conducted myself.

From my research with newly qualified teachers and trainees, I understand that you appreciate case studies within a text book and also enjoy texts that have resource lists, so Chapter 9 includes a comprehensive overview of the resources available to creatively teach RE. However, there is an added dimension in this chapter, as there are case studies and explanations on how to use them creatively. Chapter 12 also extends this to support your professional development with some of the basic knowledge you would need to teach a religion, although it is intended that you should use the information as a springboard into auditing your existing knowledge and conducting further research.

The final two chapters (10 and 11) focus on planning and assessment of RE, which some would claim are the nuts and bolts of learning and teaching. However, I believe that they are only the nuts and bolts if they have a spoke and wheel to work with and, to me, developing PLTS through cross-curricular/thematic learning are the spokes and the wheel is creativity. To be able to assess RE you need to know what you want the children to have learnt; when planning, if you consider PLTS, you will begin to see the value of cross-curricular and thematic learning, which in turn will extend into creative teaching and be useful for assessment. However, it is important to remember from Chapter 1 that there is a distinction between learning creatively and being creative.

Learning creatively is the mode of learning, i.e., how a person learns in a certain environment, whereas *being creative* is how a person may demonstrate what they have learnt through a creative method. To plan and assess well you need to cater for both forms of creativity.

I am certain that this book will have helped you to improve your personal professional development with regard to Religious Education and aided your understanding of how to be a creative teacher of RE. I hope it has inspired you to reconsider the value of Religious Education and realise that its potential benefits to children are immense. Yet the main thing I want you to have understood from this text is how it is essential that you provide opportunities for creativity and that you model it with your children so that they, and indeed you, become creative thinkers and learners because, as my creative *haiku* states:

Creativity
Works so well with RE:
Try it and you'll see!

Maggie Webster
2009

'I feel God's love'

'I feel squirly'

Both are visual representations of being filled with the Holy Spirit

References

Abbott, L. and Langston, A., 2005 *Birth to Three: Matters Supporting the Framework of Effective Practice* Maidenhead, Open University Press

Acts of Parliament, 1944 *The Education Act 1944*, London, HMSO

Allan, N., 1991 *Jesus' Christmas Party* London, Red Fox Random House Children's Books

Almond, D., 1998 *Skellig* London, Hodder Children's Books

Anderson, B., 2005 'As a post-religious society, England has forgotten how to cope with religious fervour', *The Independent*, 18 July 2005

Archur, M., 2005 *Stained Glass The Pitkin Guide* Andover, Jarrold Publishing

Atkinson, C., 2006 *Making Sense of Piaget* (2nd edn) London, Routledge

Badr, H., 2004 'Islamic identity re-covered: Muslim women after September 11th', *Culture and Religion* 5:3, 321-38

Bailey, J., 1987 *Religious Leaders and Places of Pilgrimage Today* Huddersfield, Schotfield and Sims

Barker, I., 2008 'Hands up if you like doing Yoga', *Times Education Supplement*, 25 July 2008

Barnes, J., 2007 *Cross-curricular Learning 3-14* London, Sage Publications

Beckett, W., 1995 *A Child's Book of Prayer in Art* London, Dorling Kindersley

Bell, P., 1991 *Curriculum Theory into Practice: Practical Topics for the Primary School* Part 3 Religious Education Preston Topical Resources

Black, P. and William, D., 1998 *Inside the Black Box: Raising Standards through Classroom Assessment* London, King's College

Blaycock, B., 2008 'Spirited music', *REtoday* 26:1, 50

Blurton, T. R., 1994 *Hindu Art* London, British Museum Press

Bowker, J., 2005 *The Concise Oxford Dictionary of World Religions* Oxford, Oxford University Press

Bowles, M., 2004 *The Little Book for Persona Dolls* Cambridge, Lutterworth Featherston Education

Boyne, J., 2006 *The Boy in the Striped Pyjamas* London, David Fickling Books

Breilly, E., O'Brien, P. and Martin, P., 2000 *Religions of the World: The Illustrated Guide to Origins, Beliefs, Traditions and Festivals* London, Wayland Publishers

Briggs, D., 2009 'I am the Lord of the Dance said he!' *REtoday*

Briggs, M., Woodfield, A., Martin, C. and Swatton, P., 2008 *Achieving QTS Assessment for Learning and Teaching* Exeter, Learning Matters

Broadbent, L., 2006 *Ready Resources Religious Education Book 1 Ages 5-7* Leamington Spa, Scholastic Press

Broadbent, L., 2006 *Ready Resources Religious Education Book 2 Ages 7-11* Leamington Spa, Scholastic Press

Brown, A. and Broadbent, L., 2002 *Issues in Religious Education* London, Routledge

Bruner, J., 1987 *Actual Minds, Possible Worlds* Cambridge, MA, Harvard University Press

Burgess, T., 2007 *Research Associate Summary Report. Lifting the Lid on the Creative Curriculum: How leaders have released creativity in their schools through curriculum ownership* Nottingham, NCSL

Bushell, G., 2009 'And now for an RE Blog', *Retoday* 26:2, 20-21

Butterworth, N. and Inkpen, M., 1985 *The Nativity Play* London, Hodder & Stoughton

Callaghan, J. 1976 'Towards a national debate', speech at a foundation stone-laying ceremony at Ruskin College, 18 October 1976

Cave, K., 2002 *One Child One Seed A South African Counting Book* Oxford, Oxfam Publishing

Chamberlain, A. and Northcott, M., 2009 'The Act of Creation', *Teaching, Thinking and Creativity* 9:2, 6-11

CEM, 1994 *Teaching RE: Sikhism 5-11* Derby, Christian Education Movement

Clarke, S., 2005 *Formative Assessment in Action: Weaving the Elements Together* London, Hodder Education

Cole Owen, C., 1996 *Six World Faiths* London, Continuum

Coles, R., 1990 *The Spiritual Life of Children* Boston, Harper Collins

Commission on Religious Education in Schools, 1970 *The Fourth R. The Durham Report on Religious Education* London, National Society SPCK

Constance, M., 2009 'Harnessing the Power of Film in RE', *REsource* 31:2, 4-6

Cooling, M., 1999 *Jesus Through Art* London, Religious and Moral Education Press

Cooling, M., 2000 *The Bible Through Art* London, Religious and Moral Education Press

Cooling, M., 2006 *Assemblies from the Gallery* (2nd edn) London, Religious and Moral Education Press

Copley, T., 1997 *Teaching Religion Fifty Years of Religious Education in England and Wales* Exeter, University of Exeter Press

Copley, T. and Priestly, J., 1991 *Forms of Assessment in Religious Education: The Main Report from the FARE Project* Exeter, FARE Project

Copsey, S.E and Kindersley, B., 1995 *Children Just Like Me* London, Dorling Kindersley Books

Cowley, S., 2004 *Getting the Buggers to Think* London, Continuum

CTS, 2002 CTS *Primary Religious Education Pupil Book 3* London, The Incorporated Catholic Truth Society

CTS, 2002 *The Here I am Key Stage 1 Syllabus for Religious Eduation in Catholic Schools* London, The Incorporated Catholic Truth Society

CTS, 2002 *The Way, the Truth and the Life* London, The Incorporated Catholic Truth Society

Curtis, P., 2009 'Where now after damning indicment of education?' *The Guardian*, 20 February 2009

Daniels, H., 2001 *Vygotsky and Pedagogy* London, Routledge Falmer

Davis, J., 2005 *Sacred Art* Andover, Jarrold

Devon County Council SACRE, 2001 *The Devon, Plymouth and Torbay Agreed Syllabus for RE* Exeter, Devon County Council

DfES, 2003 *Excellence and Enjoyment: A Strategy for Primary Schools* DfES0377/2003 Nottingham, DfES Publications Centre

DfES, 2002 *Key Stage 3 National Strategy Designing the Key Stage 3 Curriculum Guidance* DfES 0003/2002 Nottingham, DfES Publications Centre

Donaldson. M., 1987 *Children's Minds* London, Fontana Press

Dowling, M., 2000 *Young Children's Personal, Social and Emotional Development* London, PCP

Dunbar, J. and Blythe, G., 1996 *This is the Star* London, Doubleday

East Riding of Yorkshire SACRE, 2005 *The East Riding of Yorkshire Agreed Syllabus for Religious Education* Beverley, East Riding of Yorkshire Council

Ecclesiates, 1946 *The Holy Bible Revised Standard Version* London, Oxford University Press

Euade, T., 2008 *Achieving QTS Children's Spiritual, Moral, Social and Cultural Development Primary and Early Years* (2nd edn) Exeter, Learning Matters

Evans-Lowndes, J., 1991 *Planning RE in Schools* Bourne, Christian Education Movement

Fry, E. and Weller, P., 1997 *Religions in the UK: A Multifaith Directory* London, University of Derby

Fullan, M., 2007 *The New meaning of Educational Change* Oxford, Routledge

Gardner, H., 1993 *Frames of the Mind: The Theory of Multiple Intelligences* (2nd edn) London, Fontana Press

Gavin, J., 1997 *Our Favourite Stories: from Around the World* London, Dorling Kindersley Books

Glasersfeld, E., von, 1995 *Radical Constructivism: A Way of Knowing and Learning* London, Falmer Press

Gledhill, R., 2008 'Humanism to be taught at GCSE level', *Times Education Supplement*, 18 April 2008

Goens, L., 1999 *Praising God Through the Lively Arts* Nashville, TN, Abingdon Press

Gouldberg, P., 2004 'Towards a creative arts approach to the teaching of religious education with special reference to fllm', *British Journal of Religious Education* 26:2, 175-84

Grimmit, A., 2000 *Pedagogies of Religious Education: Case Studies in the Research and Development of Good Pedagogic Practice* Great Wakering, McCrimmons Publishing

Hampshire, Portsmouth and Southampton SACRE, 2004 *Living Difference: The Agreed Syllabus for Hampshire, Portsmouth and Southampton* Southampton, Hampshire, Portsmouth & Southampton County Council

Harrison, C., 2008 'Making every child matter: Music for all - how do we make it a reality?', *Primary Subjects* Issue 1

Hartman, B., 1993 *A Night the Stars Danced for Joy* Oxford, Lion Publishing

Hay, D., 2008 'On music revelation', *REtoday* 25:1, 4-5

Hinnells, J., 2003 *The New Penguin Handbook of Living Religions* (2nd edn) London, Penguin Publications

His Holiness Pope John Paul II, 1999 *Letter to Artists* The Vatican, 4 April 1999, Easter Sunday

Hoff, B., 1994 *The Tao of Pooh and the Te of Piglet* London, Methuen Publishing

Honey, P. and Mumford, A., 1986 *Using Your Learning Styles* London, Peter Honey Publications

Hoodless, P., Bermingham S., McCreery, E. and Bowen, P., 2003 *Achieving QTS Teaching Humanities in Primary Schools*, Exeter Learning Matters

Hopkins, P., 2008 'Who's Afraid of the Big Bad Tube?', *REtoday* 26:1, 46

Hull, J., 1990 Religious Education and Christian Values in the 1988 Education Reform Act *Ecclesiastical Law Journal* 2:7, 69-81

Jacques, K. and Hyland, R., 2000 *Achieving QTS Professional Studies* Exeter, Learning Matters

Jensen, R.M., 2000 *Understanding Early Christian Art* London, Routledge

Kinnaird, M., 2008 'Radio waves', *Teaching Thinking and Creativity* 8:5, issue 26, 3-35

REFERENCES

Kyriacou, C., 1998 *Essential Teaching Skills* (2nd edn) Cheltenham, Stanley Thomas

Lambert, M., 1993 *Religions of the World* London, HarperCollins

Lancashire SACRE, 2006 *The Lancashire Agreed Syllabus for Religious Education* Preston, Lancashire County Council

Langan, M., 2008 'Spiritual insight', *REtoday* 25:1, 21–3

Langley, M., 1997 *Eyewitness Guide: Religion* London, Dorling Kindersley

L'Anson J., 2004 'Mapping the subject:student teachers, location and the understanding of religion', *British Journal of Religious Education* 26:1, 1–13

Lauhert, M., 1999 *Religions of the World: A Collins Fact Book* London, HarperCollins

Lazenby, D., 1999 *Dottie and Buzz* London, Channel 4 Learning

Limb, S and Munoz, C., 1993 *Come Back Grandma* London, Red Fox Random House Children's Books

Louden, L., 2003 *The Conscience Clause in Religious Education and Collective Worship: Conscious Objection or Curriculum Choice?* Oxford, The Culham Institute

Mackley, J. and Draycott, P., 2000 *A to Z Active Learning Strategies to Support Spiritual and Moral Development* Derby, Christian Education Movement

Malcolm, M., 2000 *Animated Tales of the World* Warwick, Channel 4 Learning

Mansell, W., 2008 'Reality TV takes on test culture' *Times Education Supplement*, 4 January 2008

Mansell, W., Ward H., Milne, D. and Marley, D., 2008 'Take a deep breath – there's a sea change in education', *Times Education Supplement,* 11 January 2008

Matthieu, R., 2003 *Monk Dancers of Tibet* Boston & London, Shambhala Publications

Mayled, J., 1986 *Religious Topics Series: Death Customs* London, Wayland Publishers

Mayled, J., 1986 *Religious Topics Series: Marriage Customs* London, Wayland Publishers

Mayled, J., 1986 *Religious Topics Series: Fasting and Feasting* London, Wayland Publishers

Mayled, J., 1986 *Religious Topics Series: Birth Customs* London, Wayland Publishers

Mayled, J., 1986 *Religious Topics Series: Pilgrimage* London, Wayland Publishers

McAllister, A., Barrett, A., 1994 *The Ice Palace* London, Red Fox Random House Children's Books

McMillan, J., 2008 'The divine spark of music', the Sandford St Martin Lecture BBC Radio 4 broadcast 22 October 2008 22.15pm

McCreery, E., 2005 'Preparing primary school teachers to teach religious education', *British Journal of Religious Education* 27:3, 265–77

McCreery, E., Palmer, S. and Voiels, V., 2008 *Achieving QTS Teaching Religious Education Primary and Early Years* Exeter, Learning Matters

Miller, J., 2003 Using the Visual Arts in Religious Education: An analysis and Critical evaluation *British Journal of Religious Education* 25:3 200–213

Morley, J., 1998 *Look and Wonder Gods and Goddesses* Brighton, Salariya Book Company Ltd

NACCE, 1999 'All Our Futures: Creativity, Culture and Education' Nottingham, DfES Publications Centre

Nes, S., 2006 *The Mystical Language of Icons* Grand Rapids, MI, Eerdmans

Ord, W, 2008 'RE, Meditation and who am I?' *REtoday* 25:1, 30–31

Osterley, W., 2002 *Sacred Dance in the Ancient World* New York, Dover Publications

Owen-Jones, P., 2009 *Around the World in 80 Faiths* London, BBC Books

Pardue, E., 2005 *The Drama of Dance in the Local Church* Longwood, FL, Xulon Press

Pienkowski, J., 2006 *The First Christmas* London, Puffin Books

Pollard, A., 1997 *Reflective Teaching in the Primary School: a Handbook for the Classroom*, London, Cassell

Pollard, A., 2005 *Reflective Teaching* (2nd edn) London, Continuum

Provensen, A. and Provensen, M., 1991 *Shaker Lane* London, Walker Books

Qualifications and Curriculum Authority, 1999 *The National Curriculum Handbook for Primary Teachers in England Key Stages 1 and 2* London, DfEE & QCA

Qualifications and Curriculum Authority, 2004 *Religious Education The Non Statutory Framework* QCA/04/1336 London, QCA Publications

Radley, G., 1984 *Second Birth: The Goal of Life* London, Bahai Publishing Trust

Revell, L., 2005 'Student Primary teachers and their experience of religious education in schools', *British Journal of Religious Education* 27:3, 215-26

Robson, D., 1999 *Daily Express* 2 December 1999

Rose, D. and Rose, G., 1997 *A World of Faith Series: Passover* London, Evans Brothers

Rose, J., 2008 *The Independent Review of the Primary Curriculum* PPAPG/D35(3931)/1208/13

Sardar, Z., 2005 'From 9/11 to 7/7, we have come a long way' *The Independent*, 10 July 2005

SCAA, 1994 *Analysis of SACRE Reports 1994* London, SCAA

SCAA Working Groups, 1993 *Model Syllabus 1: Living Faiths Today* London, SCAA

SCAA Working Groups, 1993 *Model Syllabus 2: Questions and Teachings* London, SCAA

Serraillier, I., 1956, *The Silver Sword* London, Random House UK

Shropshire, Telford and Wrekin SACRE, 2004 *Agreed Syllabus for RE Shropshire* Shrewsbury, Shropshire County Council

Siku, 2007 *The Manga Bible: Raw Edition* London Hodder & Stoughton

Siku, 2007 *The Manga Bible: NT Extreme* London, Hodder & Stoughton

Slee, P. and Shute, R., 2003 *Child Development: Thinking about Theories* London, Oxford University Press

Spiegelman, A., 1996 *The Complete Maus* London, Penguin Books

Spiegelman, A., 2003 *The Complete Maus: A Survivor's Tale* London, Penguin Books

Stern, J. 2006 *Teaching Religious Education: Researchers in the Classroom* London, Continuum

Swann, M., 1985 *Education for All: A Brief Guide to the Main Issues of the Swann Report* London, HMSO

Taylor, S., 2008 'One size doesn't fit all'. *Times Education Supplement*, 11 January 2008

Theroux, P., 1978 *A Christmas Card* London, Hamish Hamilton

Thompson, C., 1995 *How to Live Forever* London, Red Fox Random House Children's Books

Turpin, A., 1995 'A people's guide to the Turner Prize' *The Independent*, 26 November 1995

Tynder, L., 2008 'And now for some dancing in RE' *REtoday* 25:2

Varley, S., 1984 *Badger's Parting Gifts* London, Anderson Press Ltd

Waddell, M. and Barrett, A., 1990 *The Hidden House* London, Walker Books

Wallace, B., 2001 *Teaching Thinking Skills Across the Primary School* London, David Foulton Publishers

Wallace, B. and Adams, H., 1993 *TASC: Thinking Actively in a Social Context* Oxford, AB Academic Publishers

Ward, H., 2008 'More play in primaries', *Times Education Supplement*, 11 January 2008

Watson, B. and Thompson, P., 2007 *The Effective Teaching of Religious Education* (2nd edn) Harlow, Pearson Education

West Riding County of Yorkshire (County Council), 1966 *Suggestions for Religious Education: the West Riding Syllabus* Yorkshire, West Riding of Yorkshire County Education Dept

Westell, R., 1994 *The Witness*, London, Macmillan Children's Books

Weston, K., 1997 *Granny Goes to Bethlehem*, Oxford, Oxford University Press

William, K., 2005 'A non statutory framework for religious education: issues and opportunities', *British Journal of Religious Education* 27:1, 41-52

Wilson, J., 2000 *Vicky Angel* London, Doubleday

Wirral SACRE, 2007 *Wirral Agreed Syllabus for Religious Education*, Wirral County Council

Wood, C., 2008 *100 Ideas for Teaching Religious Education* London, Continuum

Woodwand, W., 2005 'Landscape architect' *The Guardian*, 5 April 2005

Wosien, M., 1992 *Sacred Dance Encounter with the Gods* New York, Thames & Hudson

Websites

24 Hour Museum, http://www.24hourmuseum.org.uk, accessed 22 July 2008

24 Hour Museum, http://www.show.me.uk, accessed 22 July 2008

Amy Grant, http://www.amygrant.com, accessed 13 January 2009

Apple Itunes, http://www.apple.com/itunes/store, accessed 19 January 2009

Arthur Dooley art in Liverpool – Black Christ, http://www.liverpoolmonuments.co.uk/dooley/christ01.html, accessed 18 March 2009

Arthur Dooley Art in Liverpool – Religious Sculpture, http://www.liverpoolmonuments.co.uk/relstatues/main.html, accessed 18 March 2009

Arthur Dooley information, http://www.bbc.co.uk/liverpool/content/articles/2006/11/15/arthur_dooley_studio_feature.shtml, accessed 5 February 2009

Arts Council, http://www.artscouncil.org.uk/, accessed 17 March 2009

Barber Institute of Arts, Birmingham, http://www.barber.org.uk/, accessed 5 February 2009

BBC 2 Jan 2009 Around the World in 80 Faiths, http://www.bbc.co.uk/80faiths/, accessed 16 March 2009

BBC News – Muslims welcome hate Crime review 2001, http://news.bbc.co.uk/1/hi/uk/1576854.stm, accessed 3 July 2008

BBC News Channel 8 December 2008, http://news.bbc.co.uk/1/hi/education/7770469.stm, accessed 13 January 2009

BBC, http://www.bbc.co.uk/religion, accessed 22 July 2008

BBC, http://www.bbc.co.uk/schools/religion, accessed 22 July 2008

British Library Education, http://www.bl.uk/education, accessed 22 July 2008

British Library Words Alive!, http://www.blewa.co.uk/project4/children/C4_0.htm, accessed 22 July 2008

British Library Words Alive!, http://www.blewa.co.uk/project4/teachers/T4-1.htm, accessed 22 July 2008

British Library, http://www.bl.uk/onlinegallery/sacredtexts/ttpbooks.html, accessed 22 July 2008

Callaghan, J., 1991 (The Guardian 2001) 'Continuing the education debate', http://education.guardian.co.uk/thegreatdebate/story/0,,574645,00.html, accessed 17 March 2009

Channel 4, http://www.channel4learning.com, accessed 22 July 2008

Channel 4, http://www.dottieandbuzz.co.uk/, accessed 22 July 2008

Creating a mezuzah, http://www.blewa.co.uk/project4/children/C4_3_4a.htm, accessed 3 March 2009

Creative Partnerships, http://www.creative-partnerships.com/, accessed 17 March 2009

Culham Institute, http://www.culham.ac.uk/, accessed 22 July 2008

Department for Children, Schools and Families, http://www.standards.dfes.gov.uk/personalised learning/about/, accessed 8 July 2008

Department for Eduaction and Schools, http://www.standards.dfes.gov.uk/schemes2/religion, accessed 22 July 2008

Desert Island Disks, http://www.bbc.co.uk/radio4/factual/desertislanddiscs.shtml, accessed 13 January 2009

Escalate, http://www.escalate.ac.uk/, accessed 17 March 2009

Faith in Schools, http://www.faithinschools.org/, accessed 22 July 2008

Farmingham Trust, http://www.farmington.ac.uk/, accessed 22 July 2008

Godly Play, http://www.godlyplay.org.uk, accessed 26 January 2009

Google Images PlayStation Crown of Thorns, http://images.google.co.uk/images?gbv=2&hl=en&q=playstation+crown+of+thorns, accessed 9 February 2009

Google Images search engine, http://www.google.co.uk/, accessed 9 February 2009

Google Images Wayne Rooney Nike, http://images.google.co.uk/images?gbv=2&hl=en&q=wayne+rooney+nike+, accessed 9 February 2009

Hindu Kids Universe, http://www.hindukids.org/stories, accessed 22 July 2008

His Holiness Pope John Paul II, http://www.vatican.va/holy_father/john_paul_ii/letters/documents/hf_jp-ii_let_23041999_artists_en.html, accessed 19 January 209

Humanist Society, http://www.humanism.org.uk/site/cms/, accessed 22 July 2008

Hymn lyrics, http://www.hymnlyrics.org/)., accessed 20 November 2008

Hymns, http://www.hymnsite.com/, accessed 19 January 2009

Hymns, http://www.stmarysbaldock.fsnet.co.uk/hymns/, accessed 13 January 2009

Islamic Art, http://www.bbc.co.uk/religion/religions/islam/art/art_2.shtml, accessed 05 February 2009

itunes, http://www.apple.com/confirm/itunes/thankyou.html, accessed 21 January 2009

James Bulger BBC, http://news.bbc.co.uk/onthisday/hi/dates/stories/february/20/newsid_2552000/2552185.stm, accessed 22 August 2008

Kathakali dance company, http://www.kathakali.net/), accessed 20 November 2008

National College of School Leadership, http://www.ncsl.org.uk/, accessed 17 March 2009

National Curriculum Online, http://curriculumonline.gov.uk/Default.htm, accessed 8 July 2008

National Curriculum online, http://www.curriculumonline.gov.uk/Subjects/RE/Subject.htm, accessed 22 July 2008

National Curriculum Online, www.ncaction.org.uk/creativity/, accessed 18 May 2008

National Currliculum in Action, http://curriculum.qca.org.uk/key-stages-1-and-2/index.aspx, accessed 9 March 2009

National Gallery London, http://www.nationalgallery.org.uk/, accessed 05 February 2009

National Society for Promoting RE, http://www.natsoc.org.uk/schools/curriculum/re/, accessed 22 July 2008

Pearson Education, http://vig.pearsoned.co.uk/catalog/main_content/0,1151,-500,00.html, accessed 24 July 2008

Places of worship/Sacred Spaces, http://pow.reonline.org.uk/, accessed 18 September 2008

Play Station images, http://www.adverblog.com/archives/2005_09.htm

Primary Resources, http://www.primaryresources.co.uk/re/re.htm, accessed 22 July 2008

QCA G&T Coordinators role, http://www.qca.org.uk/qca_1972.aspx, accessed 17 March 2009

QCA Unit 6, http://www.standards.dfes.gov.uk/schemes2/geography/geo6/?view=get, accessed 18 November 2008

Qualifications and Curriuclum Authority, http://www.qca.org.uk/qca_13476.aspx, accessed 8 July 2008

RE Directory, http://www.theredirectory.org.uk/, accessed 22 July 2008

RE Directory, http://www.theredirectory.org.uk/journals.php, accessed 22 July 2008

REonline, http://betterre.reonline.org.uk/, accessed 22 July 2008

REonline, http://infants.reonline.org.uk, accessed 22 July 2008

REonline, http://juniors.reonline.org.uk, accessed 22 July 2008

REonline, http://pof.reonline.org.uk, accessed 22 July 2008

REonline, http://www.bishopsinaction.com, accessed 22 July 2008

REonline, http://www.refuel.org.uk/, accessed 22 July 2008

REonline, http://www.reonline.org.uk., accessed 22 July 2008

REonline, http://www.reonline.org.uk/allre/tt_top.php?3x2, accessed 22 July 2008

REtoday Magazine, http://www.retoday.org.uk/index.php, accessed 25 September 2008

REtoday, http://www.retoday.org.uk/index.php, accessed 22 July 2008

Rose, J., 2008 The Independent Review of the Primary Curriculum PPAPG/D35(3931)/1208/13 http://publications.teachernet.gov.uk

Sadar, Z., - The Independent Online, http://www.independent.co.uk/opinion/commentators/ziauddin-sardar-from-911-to-77-we-have-come-a-long-way-498232.html, accessed 22 August 2008

Sami Yusuf, http://www.samiyusuf.com/, accessed 13 January 2009

Sandford St Martin Trust, http://www.sandfordawards.org.uk/, accessed 19 January 2009

SCAA model syllabus, http://re-xs.ucsm.ac.uk/pgce/otherdocs.html, accessed 22 August 2008

Second life, http://secondlife.com/, accessed 19 January 2009

SHAP, http://www.shapworkingparty.org.uk/, accessed 22 July 2008

Simple Mantras, http://www.sanskritmantra.com/simple.htm, accessed 13 January 2009

Sing Up, http://www.singup.org/, accessed 19 January 2009

http://www.stumbleupon.com/s/#1jp8LY/villageofjoy.com/20-unusual-churches-part-i//topic:Architecture

Teachers TV, http://www.teachers.tv/, accessed 3 July 2008

Teachers TV, http://www.teachers.tv/search/node/religious+education, accessed 22 July 2008

The Independent Review of the Primary Curriculum, http://publications.teachernet.gov.uk/eOrdering Download/IPRC_Report.pdf, accessed 21 January 209 (PDF)

The Manga Bible, http://themangabible.com, accessed 05 February 2009

The Music Manifesto, http://www.musicmanifesto.co.uk, accessed 19 January 2009

Times of India 2001, http://timesofindia.indiatimes.com/articleshow/1723325485.cms, accessed 3 July 2008

twenty unusual churches, http://stumbleupon.com/toolbar/, accessed 2 February 2009

University of Cumbria, http://re-xs.ucsm.ac.uk/, accessed 21 July 2008

Victoria and Albert Museum London, http://www.vam.ac.uk/, accessed 05 February 2009

Woodward, W. (2005) 'Landscape architect', http://www.guardian.co.uk/education/2005/apr/05/schools.politics, accessed 17 March 2009

World Museum Liverpool, http://www.liverpoolmuseums.org.uk/wml/, accessed 05 February 2009

World of Glass Museum, http://www.worldofglass.com/, accessed 9 February 2009

Other resources

(Prices as at time of publication)

Granada Learning, *Aspects of Religion*, £49.00 CD

Birchfield Interactive, *Interactive Places of Worship - Christianity*, £59.95 CD

Articles of Faith, *Animated Haggadah*, £21.95 CD

Channel 4, *Africa's Child*, £14.99 Video

ATRES, *Big Questions*, £10.00 Video

Christian Aid, *Good Day India*, £5.99 Video

BBC Education, *Places of Worship*, £39.99 DVD

REMP, *Looking at Faith*, £35.00 Video

Artist Formerly Known as Prince, NPG Records, *Emancipation*, c. £20 MP3

Fischbacher, S., *Fischy Music, I Wonder Why?*, £14.50 CD

Fischbacher, S., *Fischy Music Something Fischy*, CD and songbook, £20.00 CD

Boko Suzuki 20 Bit Mastering Technology, *Tai Chi Sunrise*, £10 CD

Articles of Faith, www.articlesoffaith.com, Story Telling Doll, £31 Doll

Sunidhi Chauhan Dhoom itunes, *Dhoom Machale*, £0.79 MP3

Walt Disney, *Finding Nemo*, c. £4.95 DVD

Channel 4, *Dotty and Buzz*, c. £14.95 DVD

Walt Disney, *Sister Act*, c. £4.95 DVD

Index

EXCITING TITLES FOR PRIMARY TEACHERS FROM LONGMAN

9781405873987

9781405899505

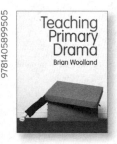

9781405899482

9781408223208

9781405841146

9781405841153

9781408221242

9781408220399

9781405873260

9781408228029

9781405835749

9781405821278

Available from all good bookshops or order online at:
www.pearsoned.co.uk/education

Longman
is an imprint of

PEARSON